# Prepared PARENT'S OPERATIONAL MANUAL

## Sending Your Child to College

D1280367

# Important Note to the Reader

# Sending Your Child to College

# Prepared PARENT'S OPERATIONAL MANUAL

by

## Marie Pinak Carr

and

Katharine Marie Carr ........... Emory University 2006;
Georgetown University 2007

Ann Louise Carr ................... Texas A&M University 2009

Elizabeth Ashby Carr ........... Boston University 2010

Dicmar Publishing • Washington, DC

Cover and book design by Innovative Projects, Inc.

Inquiries should be addressed to:
Dicmar Publishing
4057 Highwood Court, NW
Washington, DC 20006

www.dicmar.com


ISBN: 978-0-933165-10-6

Printed in the United States of America
First edition

1 2 3 4 5 6 7 8 9

**Library of Congress Cataloging-in-Publication Data**
Number 2008920846

Dear Parents,

I wish I knew then what I know now. How many times have we all heard this? So much has changed since we were in college; the laws, rules, regulations and in the helpful resources that colleges make available. There are many things that the student needs to do to prepare for college and also a lot that parents need to do and learn before they wave good-bye at the airport or dorm.

Five years and four colleges later, I have tried to keep track of everything we have learned, often the hard way.

What happens when the tuition bill is sent to an email account and ignored?

How can I help when my child gets sick?

How do I manage risks and costs in an expensive time?

A lot happens between being accepted and the first day of class. I hope this book will make the journey easier. My daughters have added chapters, comments and suggestions to help lower the parental anxiety level. Be organized, plan ahead, and make the most of these exciting years.

Sincerely,

Marie Pinak Carr

# Table of Contents

## *Going to College and Moving In*

## *Information You Need To Tell Your Child*

## *Just for Parents*

# BEFORE YOU EVEN START

# NOTES

# Chapter 1

........................................

## *Get Organized and Be Prepared*

# CHECK LIST

❏ *Create Files*

❏ *Create Calendar*

❏ *Receive a copy of your child's class schedule*

# CAUTION

Your child will be living independently for the first time and you can expect to receive phone calls about everything and anything.

Once Kate called to ask, "Mom, how do you get spaghetti sauce out of a blouse?"

Ann called when someone hit her car in the parking lot and needed to know how to go about filing an insurance claim.

Beth called asking me if I could retrieve her resumé from the computer or if I had one I could email to her. Another time, she needed to know for the BU Crew Team physical the exact days she had chicken pox in first grade!

Little by little I got more and more organized and now the most unusual request can be answered or handled easily within minutes instead of hours.

*Make copies of all documents that you give to the college and IMMEDIATELY FILE them. This includes checks and other forms of payments.*

# CREATE A FILING SYSTEM

✳ It is imperative that you create a filing system specifically for your child's college and all correspondence and materials related to it.

✳ Purchase a set of 12 pastel colored hanging files and label them: Bank Accounts, Brochures, College Guide, Credit Information, Correspondence, Housing, Insurance, Maps, Medical, Miscellaneous Travel and Tuition. Should you need to retrieve information from them and you are not at home with your files, it's far easier to tell someone over the phone to find the purple folder marked Medical.

✳ Inside each folder write the point of contact person and phone numbers.

# CREATE A YEARLY CALENDAR
# THAT LISTS...

Move into Dorms/Housing _____

First Day of School _____

Parents Weekend _____

Thanksgiving Vacation _____

First Semester Final Exam Dates _____

Semester Break _____

Second Semester Begins _____

Spring Break _____

Second Semester Final Exam Dates _____

Last Day of School _____

Date Tuition Checks Due — 1st Semester _____

2nd Semester _____

Other Important Dates _____

_____

_____

_____

_____

# STUDENT'S SCHEDULE

|  | Monday | Tuesday | Wednesday |
|---|---|---|---|
| 8:00 AM |  |  |  |
| 9:00 |  |  |  |
| 10:00 |  |  |  |
| 11:00 |  |  |  |
| 12:00 PM |  |  |  |
| 1:00 |  |  |  |
| 2:00 |  |  |  |
| 3:00 |  |  |  |
| 4:00 |  |  |  |
| 5:00 |  |  |  |
| 6:00 |  |  |  |
| 7:00 |  |  |  |
| 8:00 |  |  |  |
| 9:00 |  |  |  |
| 10:00 |  |  |  |

# STUDENT'S SCHEDULE

| THURSDAY | FRIDAY | SATURDAY | SUNDAY | |
|---|---|---|---|---|
| | | | | 8:00 AM |
| | | | | 9:00 |
| | | | | 10:00 |
| | | | | 11:00 |
| | | | | 12:00 PM |
| | | | | 1:00 |
| | | | | 2:00 |
| | | | | 3:00 |
| | | | | 4:00 |
| | | | | 5:00 |
| | | | | 6:00 |
| | | | | 7:00 |
| | | | | 8:00 |
| | | | | 9:00 |
| | | | | 10:00 |

✳ *Keep a copy of the student's schedule. If there's an emergency, you will not only know where to reach your child, but possibly which professor needs to be contacted.*

✳ *If need be, highlight calendar information with a colored marker to distinguish your college bound child's schedule and special dates from others.*

# DURING THE SUMMER YOU SHOULD

•••••••••••••••••••••••••••••••••••••••••••••

# NOTES

# Chapter 2

· · · · · · · · · · · · · · · · · · · · · · · · · · · · · · · · · · · · · · · · ·

*College*
*Paperwork*
*and Forms*

# CHECK LIST

❑ *Health Forms*

Date received _____ Date returned _____

❑ Copies filed

❑ *Physical Booked*

Date of appointment _____

❑ Copies filed

❑ *Vaccination Updates*

Date of appointment _____

❑ Copies filed

❑ *Housing Forms*

Date received _____ Date returned _____

❑ Copies filed          ❑ Receipt verified

❑ *Tuition Bills*

Date received _____ Date returned _____

❑ Copies filed          ❑ Receipts verified

❑ *New Student Orientation*

Date received _____ Date returned _____

# IMPORTANT MAIL FROM YOUR CHILD'S COLLEGE

O nce your child is accepted and you've sent in your deposit to hold your child's space, you can expect to be bombarded with correspondence and "junk" mail. Everyone will want your child to open an account with them, finance their education through them or purchase from them. Most of these items will be sent to your child who will probably ignore them *(including the* **TUITION BILL***)*.

• • • • • • • • • • • • • • • • • • • • • • • • • • • • • • • • • • • •

**WARNING** *Be on the look out for the following mail items. They will need to be opened and responded to ASAP.*

*If your child is abroad or out of town make arrangements to have all mail opened and responded to in his/her absence.* **DO NOT WAIT** *until the end of the summer or the child's return.*

✳ **NOTE:** *each of these topics will be discussed in greater detail in a separate chapter.*

# HEALTH FORMS

Start gathering all of your child's medical information in one place and **book a doctor's appointment** because your child will most likely need a physical examination and the physician's record of vaccinations and immunizations sent in before school starts. If your child has been recruited to play a team sport you should also be prepared to answer a detailed questionnaire. Beth was recruited to row for Boston University and her questionnaire asked for the exact date that she had chicken pox in first grade.

• • • • • • • • • • • • • • • • • • • • • • • • • • • • • • • • • • • • • • •

**WARNING** *Contact your health insurance company now and determine if your child will be covered while at college. If so, ask for a separate insurance card in the child's name or a letter stating that you have coverage. (See pages 32 and 37 for additional information.) You'll need this documentation to opt out of any insurance coverage fees that some colleges automatically assess on your tuition bill.*

# HOUSING INFORMATION

This information could come in a large package containing literature about the housing options, or it could be smaller in nature and direct you to the website for information and sometimes even virtual tours of dorm rooms.

*Fill out the questionnaire and send it along*

*with your deposit as soon as possible.*

*Just as in life, college housing has a pecking order,*

*freshmen are last and it's a "first come, first served" format.*

Often freshmen are housed together in the same dorms and sometimes these dorms are clustered together in the same general area. Within this selection though, there are desired rooms and locations, and these fill up quickly. It's normally a "first come, first served" format and the longer you wait to return your response and deposit, the fewer the options. Regrettably some colleges can not house all of their incoming freshmen and failure to return the form and your deposit in a timely fashion can have the detrimental impact of your child being put on a waiting list, or worse yet, not being housed at all.

In some instances there are "privately owned student residences." In College Station, Texas, for example there is an opportunity to live in either a dormitory setting called the Callaway House or a villas setting called Callaway Villas. Both are walking distance from campus and operated and professionally managed by American Campus Communities. Rooms in Callaway fill up a full year in advance. These residences have full kitchens, include washers and dryers, and are often a better value than other options.

# NEW STUDENT ORIENTATION

All schools offer a first year student orientation. Some schools offer this during the summer and others offer it between the day you move in and the day classes start.

*Immediately consult your child and your calendar*

*and then register as soon as possible.*

*There are always some weekends*

*that are more popular than others.*

# TUITION BILL

Even though you will probably be paying this, the bill will be directed and mailed to the address your child has provided. Some schools only send electronic invoices to your child's college email account. Many children ignore both the letter and electronic notice and find themselves on campus, excited about the college experience starting, and not able to register for their classes because the tuition was not paid.

• • • • • • • • • • • • • • • • • • • • • • • • • • • • • • • • • • • • • •

**CAUTION** *Read the bill carefully, there is often a charge for health insurance that you can opt out of with the proper certifications from your insurance companies.*

If the bill is not paid in a timely fashion, your child will not be able to register for classes. "A timely fashion" is determined by the university and not the postmark date on the envelope. In addition, late payments will be assessed a late fee and interest. Always make a copy of the bill along with the method of payment and date. If paying by mail, certify the letter, make sure that you have proof of delivery and plan for its arrival weeks before the due date. Colleges receive thousands, sometimes tens of thousands of tuition checks, and you need your check to be opened and processed before the due date. In addition, there's always the possibility that your payment will get lost in the shuffle or credited to another child.

**WARNING** *Your child will be adding charges through the semester to their "financial college account."*

There will be class course books, activity fees and additional spending money added to their college card. You'll need to stay current in paying these charges and many schools do not send invoices. Ask your child to check the college account several times over the course of the semester. Failure to stay current will result in late fees and sometimes interest charges in addition to your child not being able to register for the next semester's classes.

✳ *Have your child check the account for confirmation of payment and registration before heading off to the campus.*

## KEEP GOOD RECORDS —
### *this will facilitate your ability to correct any errors.*

• • • • • • • • • • • • • • • • • • • • • • • • • • • • • • • • • • • • • •

### College Payment Options

Verify the accepted methods of payment. Most universities and colleges accept checks, credit cards and wire transfers.

In case you may need to pay a bill quickly note the following:

✔ Express Mail Address

✔ Wire Transfer Information

✔ Bank

✔ Bank Address

✔ Account Number

✔ ABA Number

## Additional Correspondence you'll receive

Your child might be asked to submit a photo for a school directory or dorm room bulletin board. Before new students decide to ignore this request they should be reminded that it may seem silly, but failure to do this could mean the only photos missing are theirs.

## *It'll look like it's official and from the college but...*

FRATERNITIES AND SORORITIES WILL BE SENDING YOUR CHILD INFORMATION ABOUT THEIR FALL RUSH a period of several weeks in which students, serious about becoming part of the sorority or fraternity life, meet the sisters and brothers and learn about the Greek life and what is expected.

BANKS AND CREDIT CARD COMPANIES WILL WANT YOU AS A CUSTOMER. Remember, don't limit your selections to the mass mailings of these companies and SHRED the offers you don't want, as many guarantee immediate activation and credit.

Ann just received an unsolicited actual credit card in the mail guaranteeing $6,500 of instant credit. All she had to do was call an 800 number to activate the card. Anyone could have stolen the card, called in, spent the $6,500.00 and she wouldn't have known till the bill arrived 20 days later. In addition, the small print on the back stated that there would be an "activation fee of $199.00, annual fee of $198.00, a rush activation fee of $29.99, late fee of $15.00 — and that was before interest charges are added on. So by activating the card she would have been $397.00 in debt before she charged anything and probably not even have known it.

RETAILERS and other companies will be offering you everything from linens to gift packages to books.

● ● ● ● ● ● ● ● ● ● ● ● ● ● ● ● ● ● ● ● ● ● ● ● ● ● ● ● ● ● ● ● ● ● ●

**CAUTION** *Read the literature and consider the quality of the item before ordering. Often discount prices are low for a reason and similar items can be purchased elsewhere for the same price or less.*

*Explain to your child that the special, one-time 10% discount* ***"if they instantly open a store charge card"*** *can easily be swallowed by the activation fee, yearly maintenance fees or the interest charged on purchases paid for over an extended period of time.*

# Chapter 3

Health

# CHECK LIST

❏ *Student ID #* _____

❏ *Student Health Center at College*

Phone Number _____

❏ *Nearest Hospital to College*

Name _____

Address _____

_____

_____

Phone Number _____

❏ *Child's Family Doctor*

Phone Number _____

Address _____

_____

_____

❏ *Child's Blood Type*

_____

## ❏ *Nearest Pharmacy*

**Phone Number** _____

**Fax Number** _____

**Address** _____

**Name of any prescription(s) being taken and refills available:**

_____

_____

_____

_____

_____

_____

_____

## ❏ *Child's Eyeglass Prescription*

_____

_____

_____

✳ Plan on transferring any prescriptions before they either expire or run out.

✳ Any special allergies or medical conditions should be discussed.

# STUDENT HEALTH SERVICES

Every college and university has a student health service that is designed to meet your child's health care needs while there. Departments could include everything from medical care, behavioral medicine, crisis intervention counselors to chiropractic and emergency care. Overnight medical care may or may not be an option. Before your child is at the college it is in your best interest to ascertain the scope of their services. In addition, the prepared parent should also know the phone number and address of the nearest hospital and pharmacy.

> ✳ *Should a true emergency occur, the college will assist your child in obtaining the best care.*

If your child has special needs, you will want to discuss these needs and meet the doctors and nurses ahead of time. Ann has her own set of allergists in College Station along with a pharmacy that fills her prescriptions.

Before your child arrives on campus, every college and university will send you a student information, medical history and physical report form that will need to be completed and returned. Your child will need a physical and a physician's record of immunizations. These forms will require an *"In Case of Emergency Contact"* and also *"Consent of Treatment Permission."* In particular, it's very important to keep a copy of the vaccination record. If your child needs to see someone outside of the university/college medical system, the outside insitution will not, unfortunately, have access to these records — especially the last tetanus shot date.

*Don't forget to ICE your cell phones.*

# ICE
## (IN CASE OF EMERGENCY)

Paramedics will turn to a cell phone for clues to a person's identity. Add an entry in the contacts list in your cell phone under **ICE** (**I**n **C**ase of **E**mergency) with the name and phone number of the person that the emergency services should call on your child's behalf. It only takes a few moments of your time and you can save the paramedics time too.

Paramedics know what **ICE** means and they look for it immediately. **ICE** your cell phone ***NOW!***

# ROUTINE VACCINATION RECORD

## *Required for all students:*

| VACCINATION | DOSE | DATE |
|---|---|---|
| Diptheria, Pertussis and Tetanus Tdap or Td booster given within the last *10* years | | |
| Hepatitis B *(3 doses required)* | Dose 1 | |
| | Dose 2 *(given 30 days after the first dose)* | |
| | Dose 3 *(given 4-6 months after the first dose)* | |
| Measles, Mumps, and Rubella *(2 doses required)* | Dose 1 | |
| | Dose 2 | |
| Varicella *(2 doses required)* | Dose 1 | |
| | Dose 2 *(given 4-8 weeks after the first dose)* | |
| *OR* Varicella serological immunity/titer | | |

| VACCINATION | DOSE | DATE |
|---|---|---|
| Haemophilus Influenza *(type B)* | | |
| Polio Vaccination | | |
| Vaccine Prophylactic | | |
| Meningitis | | |
| Gardasil | Dose1 | |
| | Dose 2 | |
| | Dose3 | |

*The yellow International Certificate of Vaccination form is a convenient way to keep track of this information.*

# Medical Waiver Information

## HEALTH CARE PROXY

The HIPAA (Health Insurance Portability and Accountability Act) enacted in 1996 requires that all medical information and records be strictly confidential. As a college parent this means two things:

1. You will not be able to voice your opinion to any clinician about your child's medical care and

2. You will not have access to their medical records, x-rays etc.

Individuals over 18 are considered adults and will be expected to voice their own health care decisions and can designate a health care agent to make medical decisions for them in the event that they are unable to make decisions on their own. Each state has its own position on this and some have specific forms that must be downloaded from state websites and filled in.

If your child is sick or hospitalized **you'll need a college/ university or state health care proxy on file to direct the medical care** or to be able to speak to the treating doctor about the condition of your child.

Your child will need to fill this form out and file it with the appropriate college office and you will need to have an additional copy at home that you can fax to doctors and hospitals.

# POWER OF ATTORNEY AND OTHER WRITTEN CONSENTS

Most universities have their own form that they require students to file. Once again this is a form that your child can find in "student accounts" and can download. It is also suggested that you create and have on file a power of attorney. This power of attorney will help you access past medical records should your child need them. Blanket permission is usually not accepted, so permission may need to be granted each time your child wants the provider to discuss care with you.

You can find standard boiler plate power of attorney forms on the web if your college doesn't provide them. Most need to have a notary witness their signing and most colleges provide this service for free. Many banks will also provide this service to their customers, but you'll need to bring your own witnesses.

Ann was stung by a bee, went into respiratory failure and was transported to a hospital via an ambulance. Our power of attorney allowed us to fax the insurance information to the hospital while she was being transported in the ambulance and talk with the emergency room doctors as they treated her. Otherwise, there would have been no communication between us and the treating physicians, and we would have been dependent on her roommates. Unfortunately, the school health proxy was not accessible.

# HEALTH INSURANCE

Many states have laws in place that require all full time students to have medical insurance. Sometimes, regardless of your current medical insurance coverage, you will be billed for the insurance offered through the college. If your current insurance will cover your child while away at college, you can usually reject this college insurance and have the charge removed from your bill by filing an insurance waiver form. You may need to submit documentation to support your claim and sometimes all of this has to be done online by your child in their "student link."

It is extremely important that you verify that your insurance will cover your child's medical care away from your home area and in the state that your child will be living as a student. Many out-of-area insurance companies restrict the services they will pay for when you are away from home. It is best to inquire and ask specifically what services are covered by your insurance company prior to coming to campus.

If you have a prescription plan within your insurance coverage, inquire if out of state prescriptions are accepted. If not, you may need to arrange to have the drugs ordered online from a reliable website or be referred to a local physician.

✳ *Fill prescriptions at a drug store that has locations nationwide. This will facilitate retrieving refills in another city.*

# STUDENT FIRST AID KIT

Every dorm room needs a basic first aid kit.

## *It should contain:*

- Acetaminophen or Ibuprofen for aches, pain and fever
- Alcohol pads
- Antibacterial ointment
- Antibiotic ointment
- Bandages
- Calamine lotion
- Cough drops
- Cough syrup
- Eye drops
- First aid tape
- Hot pack
- Ice pack
- Liquid bandages
- Medicine for allergies
- Medicine for colds
- Medicine for diarrhea
- Rubbing alcohol
- Scissors
- Second Skin blisters or blister bandages
- Sterile gauze
- Thermometer
- Tweezers

# HANDLE AND TREAT

*Determine how to handle and when to treat these as true emergencies and seek immediate medical help:*

- ✔ Headaches
- ✔ Stomach aches
- ✔ The common cold
- ✔ Cuts and scrapes
- ✔ Splinters

- ✔ Nosebleeds
- ✔ Minor burns
- ✔ Ear aches
- ✔ Poison ivy
- ✔ Sunburn

• • • • • • • • • • • • • • • • • • • • • • • • • • • • • • • • •

 **CAUTION** *One of the most common causes of skin infections is the Staph bacteria.*

*Health experts advise everyone to:*

- ➼ Frequently wash their hands
- ➼ Vigorously wash your hand past the wrist
- ➼ Don't share personal items
- ➼ Clean and cover with a bandage any cuts or scrapes

# Chapter 4

. . . . . . . . . . . . . . . . . . . . . . . . . . . . . . . . . . . . . . .

## *Insurance*

# CHECK LIST

## ❏ *Car Insurance*

**New Documentation**_____

_____

**Verified Policy** _____

**Received** _____

## ❏ *Health Insurance*

**New Documentation**_____

_____

**Verified Policy** _____

**Received** _____

## ❏ *Homeowner's Insurance*

**New Documentation**_____

_____

**Verified Policy** _____

**Received** _____

# INSURANCES

There are three insurance policies that you need to check and verify the coverage on before your child heads off to college.

➤ *Each of these is covered in other sections of this book but bear repeating:*

## Health Insurance

It is extremely important that you verify that your insurance will cover medical care away from your home area and in the state that your child will be living as a student. Many out–of–area insurance companies restrict the services they will pay for away from home. It is best to inquire and ask specifically what services are covered by your insurance company prior to coming to campus.

## Car Insurance

If your child is taking a car to campus, you will want to check your auto insurance policy. Since the car will be in a new location for at least eight months of the year, this might make a difference in your premiums. It is important that the company be notified of the new address where the car will be kept. Also inquire about "Good Student" auto-policy discounts for your child.

## Homeowner's Insurance

Plan to review your homeowner's insurance policy and its coverage with your insurance agent to ensure that your child will be properly covered while away at college. Inquire if your policy will cover damages and losses due to water, fire, smoke, theft, mold or mechanical break-down. If your child lives in a dorm or commutes, your homeowner's policy should cover their possessions. Computers, cameras and other expensive items often require an additional personal article rider or floater. If your child has moved off campus, the coverage will cease and you will need to purchase renter's insurance.

## Renter's Insurance

There are many companies (that you can find on the internet) that offer insurance to cover your child's possessions while away from home. Usually the landlord's insurance will not cover the replacement value of your child's possessions should the property that your child is renting suffer from smoke, water or fire damage. It is expected that those damages would be protected and covered by a separate policy held by the renter or in this case your child. These policies are affordable, easily transferable from one location to another and the rate depends usually on the value of the possessions, the locations and the size of the rental unit.

## Personal Property Inventory

Before you pack those items to go to college, it's a good idea to take an inventory along with photographs or a video of the higher ticket items. Keep the purchase and warranty receipts and proof of purchases.

*On pages 65-69 we have provided more information along with a fill-in chart.*

# Chapter 5

## Finances and Student Budgeting

# CHECK LIST

❑ *Discuss Finances*

❑ *Make a Budget*

❑ *Open a Credit Card/Debit Card*

❑ *Open a Checking Account*

    ❑ Student knows how to write a check

    ❑ Student knows how to make a deposit

    ❑ Student knows how to keep a register

    ❑ Student knows how to reconcile statements

    ❑ Discuss with your child the risks of having credit and identity theft.

Now is the perfect time to discuss with your college bound child money management. Open a credit card and/or debit card account in addition to a checking account and make sure your child knows how to write a check, keep a register balanced and reconcile statements. For many children this will be the first time working with a budget.

▶ Help your child get a credit card now before heading off to college, teaching the financial facts that will help your child become a frugal, saving adult who will understand finances and start to establish good credit by opening a savings account, a checking account and paying bills on time. Counsel the student about the high cost of late fees, going over their account limits and bouncing checks.

• • • • • • • • • • • • • • • • • • • • • • • • • • • • • • • • • • • • • • • • •

 **WARNING** *it bears repeating*

*over and over again —*

*SAVE the RECEIPTS*

▶ If your child is an authorized user on an adult credit card now is a good time to get a credit card in your child's name, and it is often easier to get approved as a student.

▶ Your child will be bombarded with offers of pre-approved credit cards. Compare the offerings and **SHRED the offers** that you don't want. Never toss these in the trash to become a potential "find" by dumpster diggers who trade on stolen identities.

*Banks provide many different kinds of services.*

*TWO ARE: Bank Accounts and Bank Credit Cards*

# BANK ACCOUNTS

## Checking Accounts

Simply explained, money is deposited into a bank account that allows you to write checks that can be used in lieu of currency for purchases and payments. There are numerous types of checking accounts and often many banking institutions offer special student checking accounts with many advantages including free checks, discounts on purchases and interest on balances.

*Before opening a CHECKING ACCOUNT...*

- Determine the bank services versus the fees
- Determine the convenience of the location of the bank
- Determine the convenience of the bank's hours
- Can you do online banking and if so what are the fees or limitations?
- Is there a limit of checks that you can write each month?
- Is there a required minimum balance?
- Must you direct deposit?
- Is there a limit to teller transactions?
- Does it pay interest on the balance?
- Does it come with a debit or bank card?
- Does it come with an ATM (Automatic Teller Machine) card?
- Does your monthly statement return the cancelled checks to you?

- What are the monthly service charges or maintenance fees?

- Is there a fee per item?

- What is the bounced check charge?

- What is the insufficient funds fee?

- What is the bad check deposit fee (if you deposit a check that bounces)?

- Are there any perks?

## CAUTION

*Most children pay attention to the free gifts but not the hidden fees*

▸ *Most children do not know how to write a check or how to endorse and deposit checks.*

▸ *It is crucial that you check and balance your checking account and credit card accounts when your statements come in. Any discrepancies should be brought to the bank/card company's attention as soon as possible for resolution.*

▸ *It's critical that you keep all your receipts and deposit slips in one location so that you'll have them handy to balance your statements when needed.*

## Savings Accounts

These are accounts in which you deposit your money and earn interest on it. True savings accounts do not let you write checks against the money but rather you need to make withdrawals by visiting either an ATM or bank branch. You may be limited to the number of withdrawals that you can make each month. ATM transactions may or may not be counted as withdrawals.

*Before opening a SAVINGS ACCOUNT...*

- Determine the convenience of the location of the bank

- Determine the convenience of the bank's hours

- Determine the convenience of ability to withdraw funds

- What is the interest rate being earned?

- What is the minimum balance required to keep this account?

- How many withdrawals can you make each month?

- How do you make these withdrawals?

- How many ATM transactions can be made each month?

## Money Market Accounts

This type of account combines checking and savings into one. Usually you need to keep a fairly high minimum deposit to avoid bank maintenance charges. In return for the higher minimum balance you will be able to earn more interest than a traditional savings or checking account. This is not designed to replace a checking account as you're usually limited to writing five or fewer checks each month.

*Before opening a MONEY MARKET ACCOUNT...*

- Determine the convenience of the location of the bank

- Determine the convenience of the bank's hours

- Determine the convenience of ability to withdraw funds

- What is the interest rate being earned?

- What is the minimum balance required to keep this account?

- How many withdrawals can you make each month?

- How do you make these withdrawals?

- Can you make ATM transactions and if so how many each month?

## Certificates of Deposit

Few college students are ready for certificate of deposits (CD), but this is one more piece of the financial picture that your child should at least be aware of. Certificates of deposit are time deposits of money. They are similar to savings and money market accounts in that they are insured and are financial vehicles to earn money on your money. They differ in that you are agreeing up front to a fixed interest rate of return in exchange for leaving your money for a fixed period of time (3 months, 6 months, 9 months, 1 year, 5 years) with the bank or financial institution. Early withdrawal of monies out of a CD usually results in significant financial penalties.

# BANK CARDS

*There are three different categories of payment cards*

- *Prepaid cards*
- *Debit cards*
- *Credit cards*

## Prepaid Cards

These funds are already stored in the account and purchases are drawn against that dollar amount. Examples of these are store gift cards. Some prepaid cards have activation fees which will lower the available spending power on hand.

## Debit Cards

A deposit is made in advance and purchases are drawn against this money. This card also doubles as an ATM card allowing for terminal cash-access. Monthly statements show all purchases and ATM activity and are available in a mailed paper format and up to date on-line account information.

• • • • • • • • • • • • • • • • • • • • • • • • • • • • • • • • • • • • • • • •

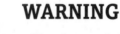

## WARNING

*Traditional ATM cards only allow you to do transactions at ATM machines.*

## *Debit Cards at a Glance*

- Can be used almost everywhere

- Usually only let you spend what you have in the bank, therefore you can't risk charging large amounts that you can't pay for

- Purchases are deducted directly and drawn down against your account's balance from your account

- Pin (personal identification number) based cards add an additional layer of protection against identity theft

- You might be able to charge more than the money you have in the account. This is called "courtesy overdraft"

- Fees will be charged for "courtesy overdrafts"

• • • • • • • • • • • • • • • • • • • • • • • • • • • • • • • • • • • • •

**WARNING** *sometimes merchants put blocks on your debit card and money. For instance if at the local convenience store you charge $5.25 — you might have a $30.00 block put on your account to guarantee payment. The $30.00 will not be available for your use until the transaction for $5.25 is posted and has cleared. An overdraft fee could be incurred if you purchase with the expectation that you had an additional $24.75 in your account.*

# CREDIT CARDS

These cards allow one to make purchases on a "loan" with the understanding that payments for these purchases will be made sometime in the future. Monthly statements will be mailed, giving you the option of paying in full by the due date or paying a designated minimum amount and having interest charges accrued and added. Current information is also available on line. Credit limits or the maximum amount of charges that you can make are preset on every credit card. If you exceed that amount, your purchase could be denied, a penalty fee can be added to your bill and you may be prohibited from future purchases until your balance is brought down below the limit.

*Before opening a CREDIT CARD ACCOUNT...*

- Determine if there are any annual fees

- Determine if there are monthly fees

- Is there a fee for cash advances?

- What are the penalties for late payments?

- Is there a charge for point of sale purchases?

- What are the charges for using ATMs out of the plan?

- What are the penalties for account overdraws or exceeding your credit limit?

- Is there a fee for using a PIN number rather than a signature?

- Can you pay online? Most ID theft takes place offline.

- Is there a same day online payment fee?

- What is the interest rate or APR (annual percentage rate)?

- Are there any reward programs that allow you to earn points for transactions?

- Do they reward for good grades and timely payments?

- What is the penalty if the credit card company receives your payment one day past the due date?

*Before leaving for college make two copies of the front and back of your child's driver's license, insurance cards and credit cards. Keep one copy with you at home and the other in a secure place at school.*

*If the wallet holding these items is ever stolen, all the information will be at your fingertips including the credit card company phone numbers usually located on the back of the cards.*

**WARNING**

*Most cards with free perks have a higher interest rate.*

✳ Is your child prepared for responsible spending within a budget?

✳ Keep all your deposit slips and ATM receipts. It's the only way to prove that you have made a deposit or withdrawal.

✳ If you plan to pay in full look for a card with a long period between payment due dates. Some cards will bill you every 25 days, but most are around 20 days.

# REMEMBER THE HIDDEN FEES

## *Fees usually are added onto your account if:*

✔ You use another bank's ATM

✔ Bank balance drops below a certain dollar amount

✔ You write too many checks

✔ The credit card company receives your payment one day past the due date

✔ You overdraw your checking account

✔ There is an annual card fee

✔ You take cash advances

✔ You make balance transfers

✔ You exceed your credit limit

✳ *Keep your receipts in a special folder and always check the credit card bill against them. Notify the bank of any discrepancies immediately.*

✳ *Some good advice when first starting out with credit cards is, if you can't pay it off at the end of the month don't buy it.*

✳ *Experts favor ATM and debit cards along with checks. Some suggest that a credit card account be opened and available to your child for the bigger ticket items like textbooks, emergency medical care, airfares, car repairs, unexpected emergencies and one-time expenses.*

# CREDIT SCORE

Once you have a credit card and checking account you'll start to build credit and a credit score. A credit score is based on many factors, two of which are the debt that you have and your history of bill paying. You can get a free credit report every 12 months from each of the three major credit-reporting agencies Experian, Equifax and Transunion through **www.annualcreditreport.com.**

One of the fastest growing areas of identity theft is college students who throw in the dumpster all their solicitations for pre-approved credit cards. Professionals "dumpster dig" for these discarded solicitations and through them can steal your child's identity.

Kate received a notification from her university saying that their student records had been compromised and suggested that everyone obtain a credit report. We were shocked to see all the inquiries from mortgage companies and immediately had her put a fraud alert on.

We also were surprised to see some "late payment notations" made by a retail store. Our daughter had no idea that these payments were late, would be on her credit report for several years and might impact her ability to obtain a car loan or a credit card at a low interest rate.

*Credit scores change all the time but bad credit history, paying bills late, or not at all can stay with you for years.*

### In brief, your Credit Score is a number based on the following...

✔ About 35% is based on your bill paying history

✔ About 30% on how much you owe

✔ About 15% on how long you've had credit

✔ About 10% on how often you've applied for credit

✔ About 10% on whether you have credit cards and/or loans

➡ Landlords, insurance companies, phone companies, credit card companies and even employers may look at your credit score and use it.

➡ When you get your credit report you will not get your credit score.

# FINANCING YOUR COLLEGE EDUCATION

College is expensive and, for many, a sacrifice, but the majority of college students today have some form of financial assistance. The best plan is to plan ahead.

## FAFSA and CSS

Virtually all colleges and universities require the Free Application for Federal Student Aid (FAFSA) and the PROFILE Financial Aid Application from the College Scholarship Service (CSS) for federal, state and college aid programs. You can look up FAFSA information and forms on line at **fafsa.ed.gov** or call 1-800-433-3243 to speak to someone who can help answer questions or fill out the form. Complete your FAFSA form as early as possible after January 1st of each year.

## Types of Aid

There are many different types of grants, loans and work-study programs that you can apply for. The Federal Government sponsors Stafford/Direct Loans, Perkins Loans, Pell Grants, Supplemental Educational Opportunity Grants, Work Study programs and the Federal Family Educational Loan Program. Familiarize yourself with the kinds of assistance available through your high school counselors, by going on line, calling for brochures from the Department of Education or contacting the office of financial aid at colleges you are interested in attending. Counselors will be able to help you understand the type of aid that will be best for you and your student.

## Office of Financial Aid

The colleges you are interested in applying to will have an Office of Financial Aid. Contact these people early to find out all of the rules and regulations you will have to comply with to get assistance. Aid funds are typically allocated on a first come first served basis. The college will require specific forms to be filled out and they will have a schedule of deadlines. The earlier you file, the sooner you will find out what your student qualifies for and what your chances of success will be. In addition to grants and scholarships, many colleges have loan and financing options that are unique to the school. Do not assume that all colleges are alike. Many programs differ from state to state. Check out each school you are applying to for their specific aid programs. It may help you make your final decision.

## Athletic Scholarships

Some students will qualify for athletic scholarships. Preparing for this opportunity will begin with your high school coach. Talk to the coach about his or her recommendations, the scouting system and the rules of applying for college scholarships. There are strict rules about showing an athlete's capabilities and communicating with future coaches. You must play by the rules to be considered for the opportunity.

## Other Loans And Programs

There are other private or semi-private student loan programs and private bank programs using family security. Remember, all loans have a cost and some interest rates are higher than others. Become as well informed as you can, and then make the decision that is best for your student and your family.

# FINANCES/STUDENTS
# BUDGETING THEIR FINANCES

## BUDGET

## INCOME

*List all income available to you from all sources.*

ONE-TIME INCOME:

Scholarships/Awards ................................................... $_____

Grants ......................................................................... $_____

Monetary gifts ............................................................ $_____

Personal savings ........................................................ $_____

Federal Loans ............................................................. $_____

Private Loans ............................................................. $_____

Other ........................................................................... $_____

SUBTOTAL ONE-TIME INCOME $_____

MONTHLY INCOME:

Salary/Work Wages ................................................... $_____

Allotment/Allowance ................................................ $_____

Stipend ....................................................................... $_____

Other ........................................................................... $_____

SUBTOTAL MONTHLY INCOME $_____

## TOTAL INCOME $_____

## BUDGET

# EXPENDITURES

## ONE-TIME EXPENSES PER SEMESTER

*School related:*

Tuition ........................................................ $_____

Room .......................................................... $_____

Board (Meal Plan)...................................... $_____

Athletic Pass .............................................. $_____

Books and Supplies .................................. $_____

Fees ............................................................ $_____

Fraternity/Sorority Expenses ................... $_____

Lab Fees ..................................................... $_____

Parking Permit ........................................... $_____

Transportation (Passes) ............................ $_____

Other .......................................................... $_____

*Other one-time expenses:*

Cable/Internet Deposit ............................ $_____

Car Insurance ............................................ $_____

Computers .................................................. $_____

Dorm Supplies/Linens .............................. $_____

Furniture .................................................... $_____

Health Insurance ...................................... $_____

Renter's Insurance .................................... $_____

Telephone Deposit .................................... $_____

SUBTOTAL ONE-TIME EXPENSES $_____

## BUDGET

# EXPENDITURES

MONTHLY EXPENSES:

*Housing:*

Rent ........................................................................ $_____

Cable/Internet ...................................................... $_____

Newspaper/Magazines .......................................... $_____

Telephone .............................................................. $_____

Utilities ................................................................. $_____

Other ..................................................................... $_____

*Household:*

Food........................................................................ $_____

Dry Cleaning ......................................................... $_____

Laundry .................................................................. $_____

Medications ........................................................... $_____

Toiletries ............................................................... $_____

Other ..................................................................... $_____

*Transportation:*

Bus/Subway Fare .................................................. $_____

Car Loan ................................................................ $_____

Car Maintenance ................................................... $_____

Gasoline ................................................................. $_____

Parking ................................................................... $_____

SUBTOTAL MONTHLY EXPENSES $_____

## BUDGET

# EXPENDITURES

MONTHLY EXPENSES:

*Recreation:*

Eating Out ................................................................. $_____

Entertainment ........................................................... $_____

Trips .......................................................................... $_____

Other ......................................................................... $_____

*Clothing:* ............................................................................ $_____

*Gifts:* .................................................................................. $_____

*Monthly Payments:*

Credit Cards ............................................................. $_____

Membership Dues .................................................... $_____

SUBTOTAL MONTHLY EXPENSES  $_____

SUBTOTAL MONTHLY EXPENSES *(from page 58)*  $_____

TOTAL MONTHLY EXPENSES  $_____

SUBTOTAL ONE-TIME EXPENSES *(from page 57)*  $_____

TOTAL EXPENSES  $_____

TOTAL INCOME *(from page 56)*  $_____

# PROTECTING YOUR MONEY

## Saving money while living on a budget at college

### *Don't Impulse Buy*

✔ Buy in bulk — especially snacks and sodas rather than using vending machines.

✔ Keep track of all ATM withdrawals and plan ahead so as not to have to make several smaller withdrawals in a month.

✔ Try to microwave and make snacks rather than eating out. Use your meal plan.

✔ Use your student discount whenever possible.

### *Watch for Sales and Bargains*

✔ Shop at outlet malls and second hand shops.

✔ Purchase used textbooks, look at sites such as

**www.abebooks.com**
and
**www.half.ebay.com**

✔ Let your computer also be your DVD player and multi-task it.

✔ Leave the car home, you'll save on gas, maintenance and parking, not to mention wear and tear.

✔ Buy spiral notebooks and other supplies at a local office supply store.

✔ Make flexible travel plans so you can get the benefits of giving up your seat for a later flight.

# COMMON SENSE

- Don't leave credit cards or checkbooks in plain view at restaurants, classes or your dorm room.

- Sign cards as soon as you receive them and report any missing ones immediately.

- Memorize your social security and credit card pin numbers. Never write them down.

# WARNING

*25-35 year olds*

*were most at risk for*

*ID Theft last year.*

# IDENTITY THEFT

## *Thieves can access your personal information from:*

✔ Stolen wallets and purses

✔ Stolen checkbooks

✔ Stolen credit cards

✔ Stolen computers

✔ Stolen mail and pre-approved credit cards that come in the mail

## *To reduce the risk of Identity Theft*

● Shred and destroy all pre-approved credit that comes in the mail to you.

● Remove and change any ID that lists your social security number.

● Don't carry any credit cards that you don't need.

● Only purchase online over a secure site.

● Don't print your full name on personal checks, print just your first and middle initial with your last name.
*(This will increase the difficulty for a thief trying to impersonate you.)*

● Don't print your social security number, driver's license or phone number on your check.

● Get and pay bills online.

# Chapter 6

## *Dorm Rooms*

# CHECK LIST

- ❏ *Check homeowner's policy for coverage*

- ❏ *Secure additional insurance riders if needed*

- ❏ *Fill in personal property inventory list*

- ❏ *Fill in inventory list*

- ❏ *Check for store sales, shop and start packing*

  ➧ Label boxes as you pack them, it'll make it easier when you load your car and then have to unpack.

  ➧ Pack the fragile items in between linens. Kate used pillows to wrap around TV and computer screens

  ➧ Office supply stores usually have school supplies on sale in July.

# DORM ROOMS

## INSURANCE/RENTER'S INSURANCE

E very year college students bring with them to college $5,000-$10,000 dollars worth of bicycles, stereo equipment, televisions, computers, books, cameras and other personal property that are at risk for damage or loss from fire, water, vandalism and theft.

Plan to review your homeowner's insurance policy and its coverage with your insurance agent to ensure that your child will be properly covered while away at college. If your child lives in a dorm or commutes, your homeowner's policy should cover his or her possessions. Computers, cameras and other expensive items often require an additional personal article rider or floater. If your child has moved off campus, the coverage will be ended and you will need to purchase renter's insurance.

## PERSONAL PROPERTY INVENTORY

Before you pack those items to go to college, it's a good idea to take an inventory along with photographs or a video of the higher ticket items, and to keep the purchase receipts and proofs of purchase.

In addition this inventory should include purchase receipts along with the model and serial numbers. Any warranty information should also be listed. This could help in recovering stolen or damaged property.

# PERSONAL PROPERTY INVENTORY LIST

| Item | Description | Model # |
|------|-------------|---------|
| Bicycle | | |
| Camera | | |
| Cell Phone | | |
| Computer & Peripheral Equipment | | |
| iPod | | |
| Musical instrument | | |
| Stereo/ DVD | | |
| TV | | |
| Other | | |
| | | |
| | | |
| | | |
| | | |

| Purchase<br>Serial # | Warranty<br>Date | Expires | $ Value |
|---|---|---|---|
| | | | |
| | | | |
| | | | |
| | | | |
| | | | |
| | | | |
| | | | |
| | | | |
| | | | |
| | | | |
| | | | |
| | | | |
| | | SUBTOTAL | |

*Use this inventory checklist to record additional personal property.*

# INVENTORY CHECKLIST

| Items | $ Value |
|---|---|
| CDs & DVDs | |
| Clothes/Shoes | |
| Electrical items *(printers, radio, hairdryer, etc.)* | |
| | |
| | |
| | |
| | |
| | |
| Furniture | |
| Jewelry | |
| | |
| | |
| | |
| **SUBTOTAL** | |

# INVENTORY CHECKLIST

| Items | $ Value |
|---|---|
| Linens | |
| Photo/Film Gear | |
| Sports Equipment | |
| | |
| | |
| Text Books | |
| Other | |
| | |
| Add $1,000 for unlisted items | $1,000 |
| **SUBTOTAL** *(page 67)* | |
| **SUBTOTAL** *(page 68)* | |
| **SUBTOTAL** *(page 69)* | |
| **TOTAL** *(pages 67-69)* | |

# WHAT SHOULD YOUR CHILD TAKE

Before you pack the refrigerator, carpet, or TV **talk with next year's roommate**. In most dorm rooms space is extremely limited and some halls do not have any additional storage space other than closets within the room. It is best to bring only what you need and to postpone purchases of any shared items until after you arrive.

* *Be advised that many residence hall beds have extended length mattresses and standard size bedding does not fit them. Some dorms now offer double size beds.*

* *Create a special box or tin where your child will always put keys, wallet, sunglasses, glasses and other essential items in daily use.*

* ***Save space by rotating clothing.***
*Plan on bringing home your summer clothing and taking back your winter clothing at Thanksgiving break. You can bring those summer items back to school and return the winter items after spring break. Parents Weekend is another good time to swap clothing and other items.*

* *Rugs are readily available for purchase in stores near campuses. I have always bought a rug. It adds another layer of cushioning, keeps the dust down, is cleaner than the existing floor or carpet and adds some color to a plain dorm room.*

The following is a list containing almost everything that you could think of to bring. Use it as a guide and once again **plan on taking only what you need**. *REMEMBER whatever you take will have to either be stored or come back home with you at the end of the semester.*

## Linens

- ❑ 2 extra-long sheet sets *(flat sheet, fitted sheet and 2 pillow cases)*
- ❑ 1 extra-long mattress pad (mattress dimension is — *36" x 6" x 80")*
- ❑ 1 extra-long egg crate pad or fiberbed/featherbed to soften an uncomfortable mattress
- ❑ 1 comforter *(washable since you'll spend most of your time on it)*
- ❑ 2 pillows
- ❑ 1 fleece blanket *(can purchase at school)*
- ❑ 2 bath sheets *(extra large towels)*
- ❑ 1 hand towel
- ❑ 1 wash cloth

## Room, Closet and Storage

- ❑ Bed lifts or rack risers ✱
- ❑ Bookcase/shelving unit
- ❑ Clear plastic boxes
- ❑ Collapsible folding crate
- ❑ Door mirror
- ❑ Drawer liners/shelf paper
- ❑ Drawer organizers
- ❑ Extension cords
- ❑ Floor lamps
- ❑ Hangars and add-on multiple hangars
- ❑ Jewelry organizer
- ❑ Night light
- ❑ Over-door hooks
- ❑ "S" hooks
- ❑ Table lamps
- ❑ Under-bed drawers ✱

✱ *Usually you have 3 - 4 dresser drawers and a reasonable size closet. You may want to raise the bed and utilize the space underneath for additional storage.*

## Cleaning/Laundry

- ❏ Broom & dust pan
- ❏ Cleaning supplies
- ❏ Clothes hamper
- ❏ Drying rack
- ❏ Goo Gone
- ❏ Iron and portable ironing board *(optional — most students will never use)*
- ❏ Laundry basket with name on it
- ❏ Lint brush
- ❏ Paper towels, tissues, etc.
- ❏ Portable vacuum cleaner
- ❏ Stain remover
- ❏ Wrinkle-free spray

## Eating/Cooking*

- ❏ Airtight food storage containers
- ❏ Bowls
- ❏ Can/bottle opener
- ❏ Chip clips
- ❏ Coffee/travel mugs
- ❏ Cups
- ❏ Ice cube trays
- ❏ Magnetic paper towel holder and paper towels
- ❏ Microfridge *(microwave/refrigerator combo)*
- ❏ Microwave-safe food containers
- ❏ Plates
- ❏ Quart size plastic bags
- ❏ Salt and pepper shakers
- ❏ Silverware
- ❏ Water filtering pitcher and replacement filters

＊ *For your late night snacks you'll want to have on hand a supply of packages of sugar, sweeteners, ketchup, mayonnaise and mustard.*

＊ *Freezer paper (found a grocery store) is a wonderful, cost-effective means of lining drawers and shelves.*

## Electronics

- All in one printer/scanner/ copier
- Backup software
- Batteries
- Cable cord
- CD-Rs
- Computer *(college may offer discounts)*
- Computer screen *(unless you have a laptop)*
- Digital camera
- DVD player
- Ethernet cord
- Extension cord
- Inkjet cartridges
- Jump drive
- Mouse pad
- MP3 player
- Power strip/surge protector
- Television
- Wireless card

## Must Haves

- Alarm clock/clock radio
- Cell phone
- Compact umbrella
- Duffle/overnight bag
- Fan
- First aid kit *(see page 33)*

## Sewing Kit*

- Pins
- Buttons
- Thread
- Sewing needles

\* *There are some wonderful hotel sewing kits that contain almost everything that your child will need and already have the needles threaded with various colored threads.*

\* *Chances are that your child will not be mending anything but every now and then a button falls off that will need to be replaced.*

*Remember that dry cleaners often can mend and hem for a nominal charge.*

## Showering

- ❏ Bath robe
- ❏ Cosmetics & toiletries
- ❏ Flip flops
- ❏ Hair dryer
- ❏ Mirror
- ❏ Over-door towel rack
- ❏ Plastic cup
- ❏ Soap container
- ❏ Toiletries
- ❏ Toothbrush holder
- ❏ Waterproof shower caddy

## Studying and Office Supplies

- ❏ Backpack or book bag
- ❏ Binders
- ❏ Book ends
- ❏ Bulletin boards for desk and pushpins
- ❏ Calculator
- ❏ CD/DVD organizers
- ❏ Copy paper
- ❏ Cord/cable organizers
- ❏ Desk lamp and light bulbs
- ❏ Desk organizers
- ❏ Drawer organizers
- ❏ Duct tape
- ❏ Glue stick
- ❏ Hole punch
- ❏ Index cards
- ❏ Invisible hanging wire
- ❏ Laptop carrying case
- ❏ Message board for dorm room door
- ❏ Notebooks
- ❏ Paper clips
- ❏ Pen & pencil holder
- ❏ Pencil sharpener
- ❏ Pencils, pens
- ❏ Picture frames
- ❏ Post-it® notes
- ❏ Removable mounting tape
- ❏ Ruler
- ❏ Scissors
- ❏ Stackable desk trays
- ❏ Stapler
- ❏ Storage units
- ❏ Tape
- ❏ Trash can
- ❏ Velcro

## Tool Kit

- ❏ Duct tape
- ❏ Flashlight
- ❏ Flat head screwdriver
- ❏ Hammer with a claw
- ❏ Nails
- ❏ Phillip's head screwdriver
- ❏ Pliers with wire cutters
- ❏ Putty knife
- ❏ Screws
- ❏ Steel Wool
- ❏ Tape measure
- ❏ Utility knife with retractable blade

# Chapter 7

New Student
Orientation

# CHECK LIST

❏ *Received new student orientation information*

❏ *Registered for:*_____

❏ *Responded on:*  _____

❏ *Payment:*  _____

❏ *Booked/reserved hotel or dorm rooms*

❏ *Arranged for transportion to college*

*Immediately consult your child and your calendar and then register as soon as possible. There are always some weekends that are more popular than others.*

Soon after your deposit is received to reserve your child's space you will be receiving information about new student orientation. All schools offer a first year student orientation. Some schools offer this during the summer and others offer it between the day you move in and when classes start.

Many colleges and universities are electing to make attendance at a new student orientation mandatory for all incoming first year students. There are optional programs for parents that run concurrently and often there are several different dates for this weekend or two or three-day orientation programs for students and their parents. Even though attending the simultaneous parent program is optional it is highly recommended that you plan on attending.

# STUDENT PROGRAM BENEFITS

These programs have been created and designed to help students acclimate to life at college and ensure that they enjoy and benefit from their initial year in college.

Among the benefits are:

- Provide time and an atmosphere that assists students in the challenging transition to college.

- Provide new first year students with a chance to physically get to know the campus, the location of the dorms, classrooms, dining halls, library, etc.

- Help students understand the various programs and resources available.

- Meet other first year students, upperclassmen and other individuals who will mentor them.

- Give students an opportunity to meet with their academic advisors, discuss academic goals and gain advice to help navigate through the academic rigors and challenges.

- Provide an overall understanding of the university and college curriculums, majors, minors and requirements for graduation.

- Create opportunities to be a part of a peer mentor group, meet others and make friends.

- Introduce students to co-curricular activities.

- Help experience a wide variety of on and off campus activities such as store runs, trips into the towns and cities near campuses.

- Create an opportunity to live in a dorm and experience the meal plans.

➧ *Sometimes certain college placement tests are taken at these orientations.*

➧ *Sometimes these sessions include registering for the first semester's classes.*

➧ *Sometimes this is the time that your child will get their photos taken and have their ID cards created.*

# PARENT PROGRAMS

While your child is attending the college new student orientation program there are optional Parent Programs offered at the same time.

## *These programs are designed to:*

● Introduce parents to their child's college life

● Give you an opportunity to meet the Deans, professors and other members of the administration

● Have an opportunity to ask questions.

At these orientation sessions your child will often be in lectures, seminars and programs designed for students, while as a parent you will be attending sessions designed for you at the same time. It's important to take notes. You will have so much information given to you that it will be impossible to remember and keep it all straight once you return back home.

# INVESTIGATE

*This is a great time for your child and you to locate, visit and determine...*

## Academic Resources

What are the available resources for help in writing papers?

What are the tutoring services available — are they free?

➡ The minute you hear that your child is struggling insist that they contact the instructor to discuss studying strategies.

➡ Often tutoring services are offered by fellow undergraduate students or peers who have excelled in the subject, for free or at a minimal fee. Quite often past exams and tests can be found in resource centers and used as study tools.

## Athletic and Recreation Facilities

Are there any additional costs? Hours?

## Banks

Where is the campus branch?

Where are the ATMs?

## Bookstores

Where is it located?

Is it the only retail option for book purchases?

Can you pre-order text books to be picked up when school begins?

Is there a used book exchange where books can be re-sold and purchased less expensively?

## Campus Map

Pick one up. Determine the location and availability of parking for future visits.

## Career Services

Where are the offices?

What services do they provide?

Do they offer workshops for resumé writing or training for interviews?

Do they offer mock interviews?

Do they help place you in internships?

## Computers

Do you need to open up a student account?

Where are the campus computer labs?

Do you get a print allowance and if so, how much and where?

## Dorms

What are the dimensions and layout of the dorm room?

Do they have single or double beds and can they be bunked?

How big is the closet?

Do they have dressers and how many drawers are in them?

What kind of desk do you have?

> How many drawers are in it?
>
> Does it have a shelf for books?

Are there sinks in the room?

Is the room carpeted?

Where is the window and do you need drapes?

Where are the bathrooms?

## Hotels

Determine the location and names of the nearest hotels.

## Laundry Facilities

Where are the laundry facilities?

Are the machines coin fed or do they use the student ID card for payment? How many washers and dryers are there?

Are the machines front loaders? This will make a difference when you purchase laundry detergent.

## Dining Halls

Where are the dining halls located?

What are their hours?

Which halls are open late for snacks?

## Dining Meal Plans

Most universities and colleges want to start students out with the most comprehensive meal plan. In truth, most students don't eat three meals a day for all seven days in the week. A better option is the flexible meal plan that allows your child to have a mix of both dining hall experiences and "dollars" that can be used at other locations.

Most students will have a student ID that can also act as a debit card. You can purchase points, dollars, etc. that will be preloaded onto your child's ID card. In some cases, this money can be used to do laundry, purchase books, computer supplies, snacks and more. Students gain access to their points by using their ID cards like they would a bank debit card.

You can usually arrange to purchase additional dollars as part of your child's account and with the tuition bills. Inquire where you can purchase points or dollars.

## Medical

Where is Student Health?

Where is the nearest hospital?

## Publications

Get a copy of the student independent newspaper.

Are there other publications?

## Retail Stores

What stores are nearby?

- Nearest drugstore
- Nearest grocery store
- Nearest coffee shop

Where is the nearest FedEx/Kinko's?

## Roommates

Ask your peer group leaders about living with roommates.

Ask for suggestions to ease the transition.

Talk about what to do if your roommate "isn't from heaven."

✳ *You may also be invited to get together with other students and their parents in your area who will be students at the same university or college. This is a great time to meet others.*

## Student Online Accounts

***Does your child need to fill out some forms for you to gain access to this account?***

Determine how to locate the following:

- Academic summaries
- Advisors
- Current class schedule
- External credit and test scores
- Final exam schedule
- Grades
- Transcript information
- Tuition statements
- Financial account summary

When and where will your child's tuition bill appear?

How can you pay?

When do they expect payment to be received and processed by?

## Student Safety

Where are the blue lights?

How do you arrange for late night escort service?

## Transportation

Where do the campus buses go?

What are the schedules and routes?

What public transportation needs to be considered?

Do you need to consider purchasing a public transportation pass or tokens?

## Miscellaneous

Look up in the phone book:

Taxi cab company

Balloon delivery service

# GOING TO COLLEGE AND COLLEGE AND MOVING IN

# NOTES

# Chapter 8

Moving In

# BEFORE YOU'RE ABLE TO UNPACK

Before you'll be able to unpack your child will need to pick up room keys and important information. They usually are given a room key, mail key and room inspection form and told how to access the building.

The schools usually have students available to help you quickly unload your car and move it to an offsite parking location. There will be hundreds of students moving in and each school has a traffic flow and parking solution that eases the congestion. Plan on moving all the boxes into the dorm, moving your car and then unpacking.

# ONCE IN THE ROOM

Inspect the room carefully with your child, making notes of any and all damages or problems. Look for chips, holes, water damage, broken handles, dresser drawers that don't slide, etc. Note this on the form and have your child return the inspection sheet to their dorm representative. If possible request or make a copy of the form. Whatever you don't note as broken, missing, chipped, etc. now may well be considered to be your child's damage when they finally leave the dorm, and it will be charged against the account in May. Unpaid accounts typically prevent registration or graduation.

✳ *NOTE: Lost room keys are expensve to replace.*

## *NEXT*

Check the corners of the rooms and closets, if you see little holes, fill them in with steel wool. They could be the doorways for little critters.

I usually use a liquid bleach/cleaner on all the counter tops, the drawers and especially any bathroom surfaces. The rooms are pre-cleaned before you enter — but a second quick cleaning has never hurt anyone.

No matter where we've been the same always holds true — **there is never enough space for everything** — so get creative, get organized, and find a place for everything. Plan on shopping for items that you didn't bring, and plan on taking home some items that there simply is not any room for or an item that the roommate has duplicated.

## Create more storage space under the bed

Plan on either racking the bed or lifting it off the floor so as to be able to use the under bed area for storage. Cinder blocks work as well as bed lifters that can be bought commercially either in stores or online. Make sure whatever you do is stable and won't easily fall down.

This is a great location to put some plastic drawer sets. These are sold individually. I find that the drawers that are housed in their own plastic box work the best.

## *Find a place for everything*

- ❑ Have a bookshelf for books

- ❑ Have a binder or shelf for DVDs and CDs

- ❑ Have folders and files for loose papers

- ❑ Box for receipts

- ❑ Plastic boxes to hold snacks

- ❑ Plastic quart bags to hold the little things like pencils, markers, sugar packages, etc.

✳ *I have each of my girls use a box, plate or some kind of small container to always place their room keys, car keys, glasses and other important items in each time they return to their room. Once a habit, they'll have a harder time misplacing these.*

## *Create some "life files"*

An accordion file or binder with pockets works perfect as a "life file." It will help your child keep track of papers that they would normally ignore. Create files or sections for finances, checks, credit card receipts, W-2 and pay stubs, medical, etc.

## Room closet

*Create instant shelving with*

❑ Canvas hanging bags

❑ Metal shelves

❑ Cardboard boxes

   Neatly cut off the top and gift wrap the outside and inside and
   place on your upper closet shelf so as the open front is facing
   you. Now you can not only fill the inside, but also use the top
   as an additional shelf to place items.

❑ Plastic boxes

   Fold your bulky sweaters, jeans, etc. and place them
   on the shelves and not in the drawers.

   Use either cardboard or plastic boxes to store shoes —
   put flats in one, heels in another and stack the boxes.

✔ *Don't use shopping bags for storage, they don't stack
and they tear.*

✔ *Don't buy super-sized baskets, tubs, or bins — they're
too deep and items will always fall to the bottom and
get lost.*

## *Create a workspace —*

## Desk area

### *MAKE SURE IT IS NEAR AN OUTLET AND ALSO INTERNET ACCESS*

❑ Have a cup holder for pencils, pens, rulers, etc.

❑ Put up a bulletin board and a calendar

❑ Write everything on your calendar

❑ Paperclip spontaneous notes to your calendar if you don't have time to write them in

❑ Have your bookshelf nearby

❑ Put small items like paper clips, tacks, etc. in small boxes

❑ Use the space under the desk for additional storage for books and supplies

## *Always lock your dorm room!*

# Chapter 9

## Settling In

# CHECK LIST

❑ *Determine method of purchasing text books*

❑ *Determine your print allowance and where you can utilize it*

❑ *Determine your college email address*

# BOOKS AND BOOKSTORE

College bookstores can be found in free standing buildings on or near campus or within the student unions/centers. In addition to books, they will also carry a complete selection of apparel, simple supplies and sometimes even dorm supplies and house coffee shops.

It's best to try and purchase your books as early as you can. Remember, everyone will be trying to purchase their text books before classes start, which will mean long lines and long waits. Be prepared to discover that you might not be able to purchase all your books, as some of your books may either be not yet available from the publisher or not enough were ordered by the bookstore for sale.

✳ *Students can spend upwards of $900 per semester on books. The university campus bookstores will be the most convenient and the busiest.*

Online bookstores often can offer better prices but remember to consider the shipping and handling fees when comparing prices. Purchasing used books can also provide savings.

**Campusbooks.com** is a good site for your child to check out. It is designed to find the lowest price of the text book that you desire by searching other bookstores and sites.

• • • • • • • • • • • • • • • • • • • • • • • • • • • • • • •

## CAUTION

*Make sure that you*
*are purchasing the correct*
*edition of the book, or consult*
*with the professor to determine if another edition*
*will pose a problem before purchasing.*

✳ *At the end of the semester you can sell your*
  *books back for cash. The bookstores, online*
  *companies and often college electronic bulletin*
  *boards will offer you opportunities to sell*
  *your books.*

# COMPUTER CENTER(S)

Most campuses have computer labs scattered in many different locations. They often have extended hours and printers where your child can use their "print allowance."

Whether it is called a computer center or Office of Information Technology there will be a support service that can help your child in case of an emergency. There are people in the computing labs or separate offices who can help with printing, the campus network and connections to the internet, e-mail, telecommunications services, etc.

➡ *Too often a lengthy written assignment is lost in a computer crash. Have your child...*

1. Save their lengthy written paper assignments on their computers

2. Back the assignments up

3. Kate always emails her papers, in their various stages of completion, to herself. If for any reason she can't access them on her computer, she can access them on any other computer through her email. This also allows her to print the papers at any location.

➡ *Most students have a paper print allowance and should use it whenever possible.*

# DORM ROOM SAFETY

✔ Always lock windows when you leave

✔ Always lock your dorm room, even to go to the restroom

✔ Make sure that you use UL-listed surge strips

✔ Don't overload extension cords and power outlets

✔ Always keep your cell phone charged in case of emergency

# STUDENT LIFE

College is a wonderful place with many opportunities to meet people and try new things.

There are hundreds of ways your child can get involved in college. There are varsity sports, club teams, artistic clubs, Greek life, music programs, religious organizations, cultural organizations, service groups, international groups, student government and many more.

In addition to the NCAA varsity sports that one can enjoy watching or being a member of, there are numerous opportunities for your child to join a club sport or play intramurals. These vary from organized co-ed soccer to sailing clubs and broom hockey and are an excellent way to meet new friends, exercise and have fun all at the same time.

Lastly, each college and university will also be host to hundreds of events each year such as sports, movies, comedy, drama, music events, debates and lectures. Quite often there are also exhibits of artifacts and art for everyone to enjoy.

# Chapter 10

*Cars on Campus*

# CHECK LIST

## *Before your child takes a car to college*

❏ Discuss the practicality of this.

❏ Discuss routine maintenance. Tire pressure, oil, fluids and windshield washer fluid need to be checked and replenished. Cars also need to be routinely started.

❏ Make a copy of the registration, date of inspection and insurance cards to keep at home.

❏ Have the car serviced before any long trips and before it goes to school.

❏ Consider enrolling your child into a national road service plan.

❏ Stock the car with a Car Emergency Kit
*(see page 102)*.

❏ Have a second set of car keys made and sent with your child to be stored in a secure place.

❑ Check with your auto insurance policy. Since the car will be in a new location for at least eight months, this might make a difference in your premiums. It is important that the company be notified that the car will be kept at another location, should anything happen.

❑ Locate a mechanic or service station before you need them. If possible, find a National Institute for Automotive Service Excellence mechanic.

# WARNING

*A car will be a distraction.*

*It will be expensive and it may*

*take away from the college*

*experience, especially in the early years.*

# CAR EMERGENCY KIT

## BASIC TOOL KIT

*(adjustable wrench, pliers, screwdrivers and wrenches)*

Car jack

Cellular phone charger

Disposable camera
*(to take photos when involved in a fender-bender)*

Emergency flares, warning triangle, or cones

Fire extinguisher

First aid kit

Flashlight

Insurance and emergency phone numbers

Jumper cables

Paper towels

Pressurized can of tire inflator and sealer
for emergency filling of a flat tire

Windshield washer fluid

## FOR WINTER MONTHS

Ice scraper and snowbrush

Kitty litter great for traction when stuck
in snow/mud

Mini shovel

# PARKING

M ost universities and colleges have an Office of Parking that is responsible for all parking lots, garages and marked spaces on campus. Your child will need to register the car with this office and purchase a parking pass. Usually passes are designated for specific lots.

In certain states, such as Massachusetts, the state law requires every non-resident student who operates a motor vehicle registered in another state to fill out and file a form with the local police station. There is usually no fee for this registration, but failure to comply can be punished with a fine. Your child can determine if the state the college is in requires additional forms to be filed.

➡ *When a vehicle is parked on a university property, there may be motorist assistance. This assistance could be in the form of jump starting your car, helping to unlock it or helping to arrange for a tow. Have your child determine if this assistance is available and if there are fees for it.*

➡ *Remember the busiest days of travel (and therefore the most treacherous) are:*

- The Wednesday before Thanksgiving

- The Sunday after Thanksgiving

- The Friday before Memorial Day

- The Tuesday before Labor Day

# ROAD TRIP

## *Before your child decides to take a road trip*

*Make sure to...*

❑ Tell someone their itinerary, especially departure dates and times and expected dates and times of return.

❑ Have the car services and checked — especially tire pressure and engine fluids.

❑ Fill gas tank.

❑ Take a car phone and phone charger.

❑ Have map and know an alternate route should it be needed. Ann writes the driving instructions on index cards that are easier to read while driving than a map.

❑ Have change and single dollar bills readily available for any potential tolls.

❑ Use common sense and safety.

# INFORMATION
# YOU NEED
# TO TELL
# YOUR CHILD

# NOTES

# Chapter 11

•••••••••••••••••••••••••••••••••••••••••••••••••••••

## *Travel and Transportation*

# TRAVEL

There will be many different ways students travel between home and school. These range from being driven by mom and dad or catching a ride with a friend to riding a bus, train, or airplane. Plan ahead with your child. Understand what the various pricing and timing options are with today's security concerns and weather issues. Sometimes a bus or train may be a very viable option. If so, know where the local bus and train stations are. Most importantly, have a communications plan. You will be surprised at what can be accomplished with planning and communications.

➡ *Make sure your child tells you his or her travel plans. Most students purchase tickets online. It's a good idea to have them automatically have the carrier send you an email confirmation when purchasing tickets.*

*Within your email system create an email folder titled TRAVEL and move travel confirmations to this folder. It's easy to find no matter where you are or if your child lost the information. Have your child create the same. This information can be accessed from any computer.*

✳ *Sign your child up now for frequent flyer programs.*

# AIRLINES

| AIRLINES | | Frequent Flyer # | Pin # |
|---|---|---|---|
| Air Canada | www.aircanada.com 1-888-247-2262 | | |
| AirTran | www.airtran.com 1-800-247-8726 | | |
| American Airlines | www.aa.com 1-800-433-7300 | | |
| American Trans Air | www.ata.com 1-800-225-2995 | | |
| British Airways | www.britishairways.com 1-800-247-9297 | | |
| Continental Airlines | www.continental.com 1-800-525-0280 | | |
| Delta Air Lines | www.delta.com 1-800-221-1212 | | |
| JetBlue Airways | www.jetblue.com 1-800-538-2583 | | |
| Northwest Airlines | www.nwa.com 1-800-225-2525 | | |
| Southwest Airlines | www.southwest.com 1-800-435-9792 | | |
| Ted Airlines | www.flyted.com 1-800-225-5833 | | |
| United Airlines | www.united.com 1-800-241-6522 | | |
| USAir | www.usairways.com 1-800-428-4322 | | |
| | | | |

✳ *Arrange ahead of time for cabs when leaving for holidays and semester breaks. Remember everyone will be trying to hail cabs on the street.*

# TRAVEL TIPS

***Before you leave for a trip make sure you have...***

★ Photo ID

★ Tickets with you

★ Keys

★ Unplug all electrical equipment except your refrigerator.

★ Empty your refrigerator of any food that can spoil.

★ Give your family or a friend a copy of your itinerary, **ESPECIALLY** your departure and expected arrival times.

★ REMEMBER AIRLINES AND HOTELS **OVERBOOK**.

➡ *Get to the airport with sufficient time to clear security. Keep in mind that on peak travel days, there will be delays.*

➡ *It is the traveler's responsibility to check the airlines web site for delays or changes in flight times. I've been on flights that have left as much as 30 minutes early without any notice from the airline.*

➡ *Get spare prescriptions and take them with you on the plane in case you are delayed and separated from your luggage.*

➡ *Print your boarding pass 24 hours in advance.*

➡ *Make sure you have a confirmed seat assignment.*

## Avoiding Jet Lag

- Stay well hydrated by drinking plenty of water and avoiding carbonated drinks.

- Eat foods low in sugar and fat content as food is harder to digest at the higher altitudes.

- Dress comfortably and get up and walk around and stretch often.

111

## Packing a Suitcase

### Essentials that will fit into one 22" suitcase

2 pairs of pants and 2 pairs of shorts

4 shirts and blouses or 4 t-shirts/tank tops

One nice jacket/tie or dress/nice pants and top

Pajamas/nightgown/nightshirt

One turtleneck

Long sleeved shirt

Sweater or fleece

Underwear & socks *(no more than a total of 7)*

Waterproof jacket, raincoat or foldable umbrella

Bathing suit

Flip-flops

Dress shoes

Cap/visor

Hairbrush, comb and toothbrush

Toothpaste, Deodorant, Shampoo, Conditioner
*(sometimes provided if staying in hotels,
otherwise purchase mini versions)*

Contact lens solution

Cosmetics

Shaving cream and razor

Insect repellant/Sunscreen
*(pack everything in leak-proof plastic bags to contain any spillage)*

***REMEMBER, IF YOU TAKE THESE ON BOARD A PLANE, EACH
MUST BE 2 OUNCES OR LESS
AND FIT INTO A QUART-SIZE BAG.***

### *Wear onboard*

Hooded sweatshirt or sweater

Sneakers/heavy shoes

## Packing Tips

✔ PACK LIGHT

Airlines are now charging fees for excess, overweight and oversized bags. Check with your airline for their rules and fees.

It's so much easier if everything fits into one 22" roll-on bag that you check on international flights and take on domestic flights as carry on. Place a label with your name and address both on the inside and outside of your suitcase. It will make it easier to locate your suitcase should it get lost.

✔ DON'T OVER PACK

You risk losing items if they can't be stuffed back into your luggage after a security check.

✔ PACK AWAY ANY REMOVABLE STRAPS

✔ PURCHASE TSA LOCKS

Use after your flights in the hotels, trains, cabs, etc.

✔ MAKE YOUR LUGGAGE STAND OUT

Attach a neon tag, ribbon or tape.

✔ LIGHTEN YOUR LOAD

Make and take along copies of the pages that you'll need from travel guides or textbooks if possible.

✔ MAKE A PACKING LIST

Keep a copy with you and continue to revise by removing items that you didn't use. If your luggage is lost you'll need a list of its contents for a claim.

✔ ROLL ALL YOUR CLOTHING

They'll pack easier and wrinkle less.

✔ PUT SOCKS INTO SHOES BEFORE PACKING THEM
Pack the shoes so that the toe of one shoe is opposite the heel of the other.

✔ ALWAYS PLACE LIQUIDS IN CONTAINERS IN A PLASTIC BAG
A precaution in case of spillage.

✔ DON'T EVER PACK JEWELRY IN CHECKED LUGGAGE

✔ DON'T FORGET CHARGERS
Pack phone, computer, iPod chargers, etc.

✔ BE SURE TO CARRY MEDICATIONS WITH YOU
Keep in their original containers.

✔ PACK A CARRY-ON
Be sure to include a change of clothing and toiletries in case your luggage does not arrive at your destination when you do.

# Chapter 12

*Odds and Ends*

# CHECK LIST

❏ *Discuss alcohol and drug use*

❏ *Discuss how to do laundry*

❏ *Demonstrate some basic sewing skills if necessary*

❏ *Discuss the practice of tipping for services rendered*

# ALCOHOL AND DRUGS

No matter what your experience has been or what your child's expectations are, if you are under 21 consuming alcohol is illegal and using illegal drugs is always illegal.

Your college or university will have a written drug and alcohol policy. It is typically clear and unforgiving. The local police departments also monitor and pay close attention to underage alcohol and drug use and have no problems incarcerating students in jails overnight for their actions. Make sure your student understands this.

Underage drinking is still a problem in colleges. Kate was an EMT and most of her emergency calls were for alcohol poisoning and related problems in college students.

Drinking will not be stopped by policies, but students should begin to understand that as they achieve more freedom and independence, they will assume more responsibility for their own actions.

# TIPPING

It's generally a good idea to explain about tipping to your child and the general amount that one is expected to give when rendered an acceptable service.

## Food Service

WAITER OR COUNTER SERVICE ..................... 15-20 percent

BUFFET ......................................................................... nothing
*However, if someone is refilling your drinks
tip the server $1.00-$2.00*

COAT CHECK ......................................... $1.00 per coat or item

## Transportation

TAXI DRIVERS ........................................................... 15 percent

AIRPORT SKYCAPS ................................... $1.00-$2.00 per bag

117

# CLEANING TIPS

✔ LINE YOUR WASTE PAPER BASKETS
Try a plastic grocery shopping bag. It'll be faster to dispose of and you won't have to deal with wet trash due to the extra drops of soda in the can that was thrown away. Better yet, consider recycling cans, cardboard, etc. both in dorm rooms and on campus.

✔ BUY ONE ALL PURPOSE CLEANING PRODUCT

• • • • • • • • • • • • • • • • • • • • • • • • • • • • • • • • • • • •

**WARNING**

*Some cleaning products that contain bleach as a cleansing agent can take the color out of your clothing if it is splashed onto it.*

✔ DON'T THROW YOUR WET TOWELS ON A PILE
The towels will mildew and will not dry. Hang them up.

✔ TRY AND KEEP AS LITTLE AS POSSIBLE ON YOUR DORM ROOM FLOOR

✔ USE COASTERS UNDER COLD CANS
Any cold container will perspire and get your papers and desk wet.

✔ ALWAYS HAVE A ROLL OF PAPER TOWELS HANDY

✳ I always use common household bleach to wipe down all the surfaces before I move my children into their dorm rooms — especially the sinks, bathrooms and their floor area. I also use bleach to wash the inside of any rented refrigerator or microwave. Make sure that you have adequate ventilation while doing this and remember to wear gloves and old clothes. Bleach will destroy your clothing and your hands along with the germs.

✳ Don't ever, ever use a dish liquid detergent *(i.e. Dawn, Joy, etc.)* in a dishwasher. You will have suds running out of the dishwater onto the floor and everywhere. Some students do not know how to load or use dishwashers. Teach them that dishwashers and washing machines only function with the detergent made expressly for them and make sure they know how much to use in the dorm or at the laundromat.

# LAUNDRY

### *A Word About Doing Laundry...*

Remember four things,

1st   Read the garment labels

2nd   Empty all pockets and zip zippers

3rd   Separate clothes into darks and lights

4th   Check all the settings on the machines and make sure **they are empty** before you put your clothes into them.

## DO NOT use hot water settings.
It will shrink clothing, bleed colors and fade some fabrics.

Leave a laundry basket *(with your name on it)* on top of the washing machine you're using. Someone can remove your wet laundry and place it into the basket for you in your absence.

➼ *Everyone will want to wash their clothes on the weekends. You can expect this to be the busiest time.*

➼ *A drying rack is helpful to dry delicates and anything that you think might shrink.*

## Wrinkles

✳ If you hang your clothes while they are still damp, they will be less wrinkled.

✳ If you hang your clothes in (a dry location) in the bathroom while a hot shower is on the wrinkles will lessen and possibly completely disappear.

✳ Shake your clothing and laundry after you take it out of the washer and before you put it into the dryer. You'll have fewer wrinkles to contend with.

## Mildew

Mildew is mold that grows on fabric. Heat and dry air will remove it.

Most often students find mildew in their laundry hampers as a result of throwing their wet towels or sweaty athletic clothing into it and waiting several days to do laundry.

# JUST FOR PARENTS

● ● ● ● ● ● ● ● ● ● ● ● ● ● ● ● ● ● ● ● ● ● ● ● ● ● ● ● ● ● ● ● ● ● ● ● ● ● ● ●

# NOTES

# Chapter 13

....................................

## *Book Your Hotel Room Now*

# CHECK LIST

## *Date*

_____ **Parents Weekend**
- ❏ Hotel reservations made
  Confirmation #: _____
- ❏ Travel plans made


_____ **Last Day of Classes/Move Out Day**
- ❏ Hotel reservations made
  Confirmation #: _____
- ❏ Travel plans made

_____ **First Day of Next Year/Move In Day**
- ❏ Hotel reservations made
  Confirmation #: _____
- ❏ Travel plans made

_____ **Graduation**
- ❏ Hotel reservations made
  Confirmation #: _____
- ❏ Travel plans made

# *OTHER SPECIAL DAYS*

## *Date*

_____ **Athletic Event** _____

  ❑ **Hotel reservations made**

  **Confirmation #:** _____

  ❑ **Travel plans made**


_____ **Athletic Event** _____

  ❑ **Hotel reservations made**

  **Confirmation #:** _____

  ❑ **Travel plans made**


_____ **Athletic Event** _____

  ❑ **Hotel reservations made**

  **Confirmation #:** _____

  ❑ **Travel plans made**


_____ **Athletic Event** _____

  ❑ **Hotel reservations made**

  **Confirmation #:** _____

  ❑ **Travel plans made**

# HOTEL WEBSITES

Best Western ........................ www.bestwestern.com

Candlewood Suites .............. www.ichotelsgroup.com

Courtyard ............................ www.marriott.com

Crowne Plaza ....................... www.ichotelsgroup.com

Doubletree Hotels ............... www.doubletree.com

Embassy Suites .................... www.embassysuites.com

Fairfield Inn .......................... www.marriott.com

Hilton ................................... www.hilton.com

Holiday Inn .......................... www.ichotelsgroup.com

Hotel Indigo ........................ www.ichotelsgroup.com

Hyatt .................................... www.hyatt.com

InterContinental ................... www.ichotelsgroup.com

Marriott ............................... www.marriott.com

Radisson .............................. www.radisson.com

Ramada ................................ www.ramada.com

Residence Inn ...................... www.marriott.com

Sheraton .............................. www.starwoodhotels.com

Springhill Suites ................... www.marriott.com

Staybridge Suites ................. www.ichotelsgroup.com

Westin .................................. www.starwoodhotels.com

Wyndham Hotels ................. www.wyndham.com

# FAVORITE CAMPUS HOTELS

Take the business cards of hotels that you like and tape them onto the allocated spaces below and on the next couple of pages. If business cards aren't available cut off the address and contact information from a piece of stationery or bill.

Hotel Name _____

Address _____

_____

Phone (toll-free) _____

Phone (direct) _____

Parking Available? ❑ YES   ❑ NO   Cost: _____

• • • • • • • • • • • • • • • • • • • • • • • • • • • • • • • • • • • • • • • •

✳ *Inquire as to available parking*
*and costs incurred to use it*

Hotel Name _____

Address _____

_____

Phone (toll-free) _____

Phone (direct) _____

Parking Available? ❑ YES ❑ NO Cost: _____

● ● ● ● ● ● ● ● ● ● ● ● ● ● ● ● ● ● ● ● ● ● ● ● ● ● ● ● ● ● ● ● ● ● ● ● ● ● ● ● ● ●

Hotel Name _____

Address _____

_____

Phone (toll-free) _____

Phone (direct) _____

Parking Available? ❑ YES   ❑ NO   Cost: _____

● ● ● ● ● ● ● ● ● ● ● ● ● ● ● ● ● ● ● ● ● ● ● ● ● ● ● ● ● ● ● ● ● ● ● ● ● ● ●

PASTE BUSINESS
CARD HERE

# AIRLINES

| AIRLINES | | Frequent Flyer # | Pin # |
|---|---|---|---|
| Air Canada | www.aircanada.com<br>1-888-247-2262 | | |
| AirTran | www.airtran.com<br>1-800-247-8726 | | |
| American Airlines | www.aa.com<br>1-800-433-7300 | | |
| American Trans Air | www.ata.com<br>1-800-225-2995 | | |
| British Airways | www.britishairways.com<br>1-800-247-9297 | | |
| Continental Airlines | www.continental.com<br>1-800-525-0280 | | |
| Delta Air Lines | www.delta.com<br>1-800-221-1212 | | |
| JetBlue Airways | www.jetblue.com<br>1-800-538-2583 | | |
| Northwest Airlines | www.nwa.com<br>1-800-225-2525 | | |
| Southwest Airlines | www.southwest.com<br>1-800-435-9792 | | |
| Ted Airlines | www.flyted.com<br>1-800-225-5833 | | |
| United Airlines | www.united.com<br>1-800-241-6522 | | |
| USAir | www.usairways.com<br>1-800-428-4322 | | |
| | | | |

# AUTOMOBILE RENTALS

| COMPANY | Website | Phone |
| --- | --- | --- |
| Alamo | www.alamo.com | 1-800-327-9633 |
| Avis | www.avis.com | 1-800-331-1212 |
| Budget | www.budget.com | 1-800-527-0700 |
| Dollar | www.dollar.com | 1-800-800-4000 |
| Enterprise | www.enterprise.com | 1-800-736-8222 |
| Hertz | www.hertz.com | 1-800-654-3131 |
| National | www.nationalcar.com | 1-800-227-7368 |
| Thrifty | www.thrifty.com | 1-800-367-2277 |
|  |  |  |

# TRAINS

**Amtrak**

www. amtrak.com • 1-800-523-8720

# TAXIS

Company Name_____

Phone Number _____

# FAVORITE RESTAURANTS

Name _____

Address _____

Phone _____


Name _____

Address _____

Phone _____


Name _____

Address _____

Phone _____

PASTE BUSINESS
CARDS HERE

# Chapter 14

● ● ● ● ● ● ● ● ● ● ● ● ● ● ● ● ● ● ● ● ● ● ● ● ● ● ● ● ● ● ● ● ● ● ● ● ● ● ● ● ●

## *Sending Items to Your Child*

# CHECK LIST

## *Address and Phone Number*

### Where packages can be sent:

_____

_____

Phone
_____

### Where Saturday or Sunday next day mail can be sent and RECEIVED

_____

_____

Phone
_____

### Nearest FedEx/Kinko's:

_____

_____

Phone
_____

## *List of Special Occasions*

_____

_____

_____

_____

_____

_____

## *Supplies*

❏ *Address labels*

❏ *Boxes*

❏ *Commercial grade tape*

❏ *Contents* (food, etc.)

# MAIL

E very campus utilizes a different mail system. Often mail and packages are delivered to a "mail room" and the mail is put into individual student's mail boxes. Notices of special packages that require signatures or are too large for the box, and are kept somewhere else for pick up, will be placed in the mailbox. Often, if a signature is required, your child will need to make arrangements to sign the release before the letter/package can be picked up.

The individual mail boxes are available to the students 24/7 however the mail room, which holds the larger packages and all signature-required items, often is open only during normal business hours.

➡️ *Most campuses are set up so you can't send items directly to your child's dorm but rather to their mailbox number at the campus mail room.*

## Express Mail/Packages

If you need to get something to your child in a hurry consider other arrangements now, before you need to send something. Keep in mind the facility and the location and hours it will be open for your child to retrieve your package. Many students are in classes when the mail centers are open.

➡️ *The arrangement that works best for Beth who is at Boston University is to Federal Express any items that she needs instantly from the FedEx/Kinko's in Washington, DC to the FedEx/Kinko's facility on campus. They're open longer hours on the weekends, and are easy walking distance from her room. This allows for the package to be delivered the next day, it's traceable, and Beth can pick it up at her convenience.*

➡️ *Even when I check "no signature required" — it is all too often ignored and my daughters still need to sign.*

# PACKAGES

Students love to receive mail and packages in addition to text messages and emails. In particular, an unexpected package of goodies from home during the stressful times helps make a student's day.

When sending boxes always do it in a fashion that allows you to trace the package should it be lost in transit. Most carriers will send shipment dates and expected delivery confirmations via email to you that can be forwarded to the student.

The contents of the boxes that I send are always a surprise, but I inform my daughters of their expected delivery dates.

*You'll want to send packages for the following reasons:*

1.  Most students are without a car and purchasing snack items will be both inconvenient and expensive as they'll be visiting local campus retail establishments.

2.  They'll make friends. When packages from home arrive, students share the goodies with all their roommates and friends.

3.  You won't want your child to be the only one not receiving a package especially at exam time. There are commercial firms that will be soliciting your business for sending packages to your child. This is your time to shine and provide something bigger and better for less money.

4.  It'll give your child a reason to call you. Simply text or email the message *"CALL ME BOUT PKG U RECVED"* They'll be calling you about "WHAT PACKAGE?"

## When to send packages

★ First semester exams

★ Second semester exams

★ Long holiday weekends that they are spending at school

★ Birthdays

★ Special award days

★ Dates of project or long paper completion

★ In honor of academic excellence

★ The day before a big athletic competition

Several companies offer you the chance to purchase a series of care packages that they pre-pack and send to your child. You simply place your order for the packages or goodies that you wish for your child to receive in advance along with the desired delivery date. Compare the contents of the packages that these companies offer to send. You can often save money, send more items and have fun doing it yourself.

✳ *At the very least try to send a minimum of three packages during your child's school year.*

✳ *For the last five years I have tried to send one package each month to each child. I plan ahead. I get just as much joy out of packing and sending the boxes as my daughters do in receiving them.*

138

## Purchasing for packages

You can create wonderful packages at a fraction of the cost if you shop prudently.

1. Purchase large containers of items at the big box warehouse stores or discount stores. Plan on using these goodies in several boxes over several months.

2. Shop the grocery store sales. If granola bars are on sale buy them and save for your next package.

3. Purchase candies and gift items at the after holiday sales.

   ✽ *I purchase dozens of bags of the green and red foil covered chocolates at the Christmas holiday sales. I separate them into piles of silver foil, red foil and green foil. I use the silver foil covered candies for any box, the red foil covered for the February box and the green foil covered for the March box. Just be sure there aren't any holiday pictures on the candies before you buy them.*

4. Plan on purchasing holiday lights when they're on sale.

   ✽ *I send white lights in December, red lights in February and green lights in March.*

5. Plan on purchasing many boxes of brownie mixes, boxes of rice cereal and marshmallows when they're on sale usually in late August and again in November.

6. Many craft stores and general merchandise stores now have bins near the checkout registers that contain items that sell for 50 cents to one dollar. You can usually find little magnetic frames, soaps, bubble baths, squirt guns, yo-yos etc.

7.  The electronic stores have weekly DVD specials. Quite often you can select from dozens of DVDs for $4.99. Around Halloween you can expect to find the "scary movies," and in February the "romances." The Sunday newspaper's circular ads will give you this information. I always have a couple of DVDs on hand in case one of the children is feeling stressed, low in spirits or sick. They're easy to send and sometimes are just what the doctor ordered.

    \*  *The sale DVDs can be purchased on site in the stores and online. Also, inquire if you can't locate the DVDs that you want in the sale bin there are often more in other locations within the store.*

    \*  *Remember, DVDs can be watched on student laptops.*

8.  Office supply stores often have school supplies on sale. Highlighters, sticky notepads and index cards are something every student is always in need of.

    \*  *I purchase the ink cartridges for my daughters' printers from Quill. The cost of the cartridges is usually sufficient to guarantee free delivery to their dorm and Quill usually has some promotional gift item that is included for free with the purchase. In addition to the ink cartridges my girls have received tool kits, DVDs and candy courtesy of Quill.*

*A roll of quarters is always welcome*
*for use in vending machines,*
*laundry machines, parking meters, etc.*

# SUPPLIES YOU'LL NEED

## ● Boxes

Plan on saving and recycling the boxes that you receive. I prefer to use the Priority Mail Flat Rate Boxes obtained from the United States Post Office. You can order supplies online from **www.USPS.com**. There are two sizes of flat rate boxes and you can pack as much weight as you can fit into these boxes. You can also pay online, print labels and request a free package pickup.

## ● Commercial grade tape

## ● Tissue paper, gift wrap or wax paper

## ● Address labels

Make several labels with your child's address on them at the same time and save the extras noting if it is a post office box or dormitory mail box. This will make a difference in shipping methods. The U.S. Post Office can only receive packages mailed through them.

## ● Fillers

*These are the items that you'll want to have on hand to fill in the empty spaces when packing your box:*

■ One container of 180 individually wrapped licorice pieces will cost about 4 cents per piece.

■ One box of 24 of the hundred calorie snack packs will cost about 35 cents a piece

■ One box of 60 granola bars will cost about 20 cents each

■ One bag of hard candies will cost about 1 cent each.

141

## Food items

Bagels

Brownies

Candy *(in warmer climates avoid chocolates)*

Cookies

Crackers

Drink mixes

Dry cereal

Granola bars

Gum

Instant oatmeal and cereal bowls

Instant soups

Licorice sticks

Marshmallows

Microwave macaroni and cheese

Nacho chips

Peanut butter

Peanuts and other nuts

Pop tarts

Popcorn *(microwave bags)*

Raisins

Rice cakes

Salsa

Snack food favorites

## Fun items

Bubbles

Desk top games

DVDs

Dorm room survival items: 6 in 1 screwdriver, travel-size containers

Halloween decorations

Holiday lights and garlands

Inflatable beach ball

Key chains

Magazines

Magnetic frames

Play Doh

Roll of quarters

Rubber duck

Sewing kits

Slinky

Small games

Small puzzle books: Sudoko, crossword, word search *(found in displays near store check-out registers)*

Small sized books *(3" x 5")*

Soaps

Stuffed animal

Squirt guns

Yo-yos

# MONTHLY CARE PACKAGES

Each month I send a box that has a theme and is filled with different purchases and home made treats and designed to coincide with a holiday or special occasion. Often these boxes and their contents cost me less than $20.00.

## Samples

Not including postage, for less than $10.00 you could send:

★ One $4.99 DVD ............................................. $4.99

★ 2 batches of brownies .................................... $3.00
   *(purchased on sale for $1.50 a box)*

★ 5 packages of instant ramen noodles .......... $1.00
   *(purchased on sale for 20 cents each)*

You can add in the following and your care package will be chock full and cost less than $20.00.

★ Add in two items found in the $1.00 bin ..... $2.00
   *(soap, beach ball)*

★ 50 licorice sticks ............................................ $2.00

★ 10 granola bars .............................................. $2.00

★ 10 snack packs .............................................. $3.50

## Additional Possible Themes

★ All night exam boxes

★ Sugar, Sugar, Sugar

# September

## *Occasion / Theme: First Month in College — FUN*

*Box / Container:* Box containing a nalgene water bottle filled with hard candies

*Filler:* Individually wrapped hard candies and licorice

*Toy / Fun Items:* Two small $1.00 items and a magazine

*Home Baked Treats:* Two batches and/or boxes of brownies, marshmallow crispy rice cereal treats

*Food Items:* Granola bars, snack packs and instant ramen noodle packages

# October

## *Occasion / Theme: Halloween*

*Box / Container:* Plastic pumpkin or trick or treat bag

*Filler:* Halloween theme candies *(avoid chocolates if shipping to a warm climate)*

*Toy / Fun Items:* Wig, mask, Halloween lights *(college students love lights to string around their windows or room)* and synthetic spider webs

*Home Baked Treats:* Crispy rice cereal treats with candy corn on top and cookies

*Food Items:* Specially marked bags of Halloween pretzels

✳ Crispy rice cereal treats are easy to make and loved by everyone. Recipes can be found on cereal boxes. I usually double the recipe and cut the treats 3" x 3" x 2" deep.

# November

## *Occasion / Theme: Mid-Semester*

*Box / Container:* Box lined with tissue paper

*Filler:* Instant hot chocolate packages and tea bags

*Toy / Fun Items:* Coffee shop gift card and travel coffee mug

*Home Baked Treats:* Crispy rice cereal treat with fall sugar candies on top and brownies

*Food Items:* Tea bags — especially herbal and medicinal teas, instant hot chocolate packages, small marshmallows for hot chocolate and packages of microwaveable popcorn

• • • • • • • • • • • • • • • • • • • • • • • • • • • • • • • • • • • • • • •

## ⚠ CAUTION

*Many hands will be touching your homemade cookies, brownies, etc. Wrap each individually in plastic wrap or in a plastic bag.*

✻ **Remember allergies — you might need to send gluten free or peanut free boxes.**

# December

## *Occasion/Theme: Exam Studying Box*

*Box/Container:* Fun looking tin or plastic container

*Filler:* Individually wrapped licorice

*Toy/Fun Items:* Yo-yo, holiday lights, stress reliever ball and stuffed animal

*Home Baked Treats:* Crispy rice cereal treats with either white/ peppermint chipped chocolate or baking chips on top and brownies

*Food Items:* Granola bars and lots of different snacks and sweets that will be consumed while studying...

- Small packages of cookies, snacks, sweets
- Instant soup packages
- Small containers of tuna fish, cheese and crackers, etc.
- Packages/boxes of instant soups that just need hot water added
- Packages of microwaveable macaroni and cheese
- Packages of microwave popcorn
- Packages of dried fruit

# January

## *Occasion/Theme: Back to School*

I usually order a five pound box of fresh oranges/grapefruits to be sent to my daughters from

Sun Harvest Citrus: 1-800 -743-1480

# February

## *Occasion / Theme: Valentine's Day*

*Box / Container:* Box lined with red tissue paper

*Filler:* Red foil covered chocolate candies *(purchased on sale in December see page 139)*

*Toy / Fun Items:* Package of cute Valentine's day cards, small electronic game, socks, red lights, DVD

*Home Baked Treats:* Crispy rice cereal treats with cinnamon candies or candy hearts on top

*Food Items:* Assortment of Valentine candies

# March

## *Occasion / Theme: St. Patrick's Day*

*Box / Container:* Box lined with green tissue paper

*Filler:* Green foil covered chocolates *(purchased on sale in December see page 139)*

*Toy / Fun Items:* Anything for St Patrick's Day — hats, glasses, garland, green lights

*Home Baked Treats:* Cookies and brownies

*Food Items:* Soups that are either instant or come in a microwaveable bowl, salt and pepper shakers and a box of crackers

## April

*Occasion / Theme: Springtime / Beach Related Fun Items*

*Box / Container:* Child's sand bucket with shovel

*Filler:* Lollipops

*Toy / Fun Items:* Flip flops, beach balls, squirt guns

*Home Baked Treats:* Crispy rice cereal treats with chocolate on top

*Food Items:* Pre-packaged snacks

## May

*Occasion / Theme: Exam Studying Box*

*Box / Container:* Tin filled with goodies

*Filler:* Bubble gum, sweets and other snacks

*Toy / Fun Items:* Send tape, labels and magic markers for boxing items to take back home

*Home Baked Treats:* Cookies

*Food Items:* Pre-packaged snacks and popcorn

✳ *College students seem to be impressed with size. I cut the brownies to be at least two inch squares and bag 2-3 cookies at a time.*

# Chapter 15

## Additional Information

# PARENT COUNCILS AND OTHER VOLUNTEER OPPORTUNITIES

There are many ways parents can be involved in their child's college.

*Some examples are:*

- Join the parent groups

- Become "college ambassadors" serving as a resource for other parents in the same geographic area

- Host send-off parties in your area for first year students

- Host luncheons for university administrators when they visit your location

- Help the university career center place graduates in new jobs

- Join the development staff and participate in phone-a-thons to encourage fellow parents to support the university

➡ *Texas A & M has 126 regional Aggie Mother's Clubs that are an excellent way to support the students while forming friendships and becoming familiar with the university.*

# PARENT SUPPORT GROUPS

## Empty Nest Support Services

**www.emptynestsupport.com** is a wonderful resource to help you navigate the road and its challenges while experiencing the empty nest syndrome. It offers a chat room, free newsletter, articles, blogs and much more.

Ask for the brochure 20 *Tips for Parents Traveling the Empty Nest Road* by Natalie Caine.

# PARENTS WEEKEND

Every college will host a Parent Weekend which is usually one of the most popular weekends of the school year. Family/Parent Weekend gives you the chance to visit with your child and experience life on campus. There is something for everyone with events, activities and programs ranging from lectures and receptions with faculty to performances, jazz brunches and tours. Some colleges let you attend a class and others offer lunch with the students in the dining hall. It's the perfect opportunity for you to see what your child has been doing since you last saw them.

Local hotels book quickly for these weekends. In Texas, Boston, and Atlanta I book almost a year in advance. Most of the information and schedules will be posted online and require RSVPs and reservations.

➡ *RSVP early. Often tickets for the musical student productions are sold out quickly.*

151

*Confirm a scheduled phone time with your child. For example they will call home every Sunday at 3 P.M. — and if they can't call home then they will notify you and plan an alternate time.*

# TEXT MESSAGING

Learn to text message on your phone. If necessary have your child teach you how to do so. Pre–arrange that they will either call or text when they board planes, arrive at airports, visit friends, etc.

*If this is your first time text messaging here are some tips:*

★ Simplify — be brief with your messages

★ Skip as many vowels as you can

★ Common abbreviations:

B .............. be
B4 ............ before
BTW ........ by the way
IMO ......... in my opinion
LOL ......... laughing out loud
OTOH ..... on the other hand
POS ........ parent over shoulder
RE ............ regarding
U .............. you
W8 ........... wait

# Chapter 16

. . . . . . . . . . . . . . . . . . . . . . . . . . . . . . . . .

## *Wonderful, Useful Websites*

## Academic

www.picaprof.com — *lists all the class grade averages and peer reviews about each professor for courses.*

www.Pubmed.com — *good scientific journal search webpage*

www.m-w.com *online dictionary/thesaurus*

www.wikipedia.org

> \* *Wikipedia, is a website that allows visitors to list and change information posted for viewers. Thus NOT ALL THE INFORMATION POSTED IS CORRECT. It should not be used a reference or source due to its discrepancies. Professors have failed students for listing this website as a source for papers and various other written projects!*

www.findarticles.com — *general article search engine*

www.sparknotes.com — *lists great study guides and online quizzes to help test your knowledge of the material*

www.ratemyprofessors.com

### *Newspaper websites also are great academic resources:*

www.washingtonpost.com

www.nypost.com

www.cnn.com

## E- Cards

www.hallmark.com — *Hallmark Cards*

www.Americangreetings.com

## Friendship /Personal

www.facebook.com

www.myspace.com

## Gifts/Shopping

www.amazon.com — *Amazon*

www.ebay.com — *Ebay*

www.1800flowers.com

www.pajamagram.com

✳ *All major department stores have online websites for shopping and purchasing items from all departments.*

## Office Supplies

www.staples.com — *Staples Office Supplies*

www.quillcorp.com — *Quill Office Supplies free shipping on orders over $45.00*

www.sunharvestcitrus.com — *Florida citrus fruit*

## Photo sharing

www.facebook.com

www.webshots.com

www.flickr.com

www.shutterfly.com

## Music

www. Pandora.com — *a free online radio website, which allows you to customize your playlist by song or artist*

www.YouTube.com

www.itunes.com

## Support Groups

www.emptynestsupport.com — *Empty Nest Support Services*

## Textbooks

www.Campusbooks.com — *Campus Books*

www.amazon.com — *Amazon*

www.abebooks.com

www.half.ebay.com

## Travel

www.weather.com — *is good for local weather*

www.statravel.com — *this student travel organization will help students find and book low cost airfare, rail passes, accommodations, etc.*

## Tutoring

*Textbook publishing companies usually list supportive websites that contain practice problems and supplemental chapter notes for each textbook. Simply check inside the front covers to find the listed websites.*

*Find local tutoring companies that offer group and single tutoring hours.*

# Chapter 17

## Understanding the College Language

**Academic advisor:** Your academic advisor is some one chosen by the university to guide your course selection. You may have a general academic advisor chosen for you when you enter college. However, once you have selected your designated major, you can often request a new academic advisor in your major field.

**Academic probation:** Occurs when your term or semester GPA falls below a set minimum value, which varies per academic institution. Typically one is expected to meet with counselors and advisors to develop a plan to improve one's GPA by the end of the next semester. If academic performance is not improved by the end of the probation period, expulsion occurs.

**Bid:** One way of requesting courses is through the bid system. First you need to decide which classes you plan on trying to take the following semester. The next step is to rank these courses — typically the smaller classes, which are harder to get into are given higher preference. Next you allocate your BID points among the courses, with the higher preference given more points. BID points are allocated to each student according to a variety of factors, including your year in college. Seats in classes are given to students according to who placed the most BID points on a selected class. However, students should know that often you have preference in a course in your designated major and as an upperclassman.

**Blue light phone:** Blue light phones are safety features on college campuses. The blue light indicates that the phone can be used to directly call campus police by pushing the designated button.

**Campus police:** Each campus has its own police force to help ensure the safety of students and the surrounding community. Students should be aware that campus police can issue parking tickets and other motor vehicle violation tickets. If a student fails to pay tickets issued by the campus police prior to graduation, a student's diploma can be withheld.

**Club sports:** Club sports are another way for students to get involved on campus. Anyone can join a club sports team and practices are often coordinated by the student members of the club sports team. Teams can compete against other club sports teams and other university teams.

**Dual majors:** Refers to students who choose to complete two majors during their college career. Students need to make sure that they declare both majors and have the appropriate academic advisors in each field. Your major academic advisors may need to sign off that you have completed the appropriate courses in order to receive your degree.

**Freshman fifteen:** The freshman fifteen refer to the 15 pounds that some students may gain during their first year of college. However, this can easily be avoided by eating a healthy, well-balanced diet and exercising.

**Graduate Student:** Refers to any student returning to college to pursue advanced course work.

**Greek life:** Greek life refers to the fraternities and sororities that are present on a college campus. Greek life also refers to the activities that these Greek organizations coordinate on campus.

**GPA:** Grade point averages are computed by dividing the number of grade honor points earned by the number of credits.

**Hazing:** Hazing is the tests and activities that are part of one's initiation into an social organization. Most often people think that hazing occurs in Greek life, however it can occur in any social organization at a university.

**Intramural sports:** Intramural (IM) sports are university sponsored sports leagues, which are available to any student. However, students are required to register with the IM league as a team and may have to pay a small fee to participate. The IM league then coordinates games and playoffs. Practices are determined by the teams themselves.

**Major:** A major is your main field of study, for which you will be awarded a degree.

**Minor:** A minor is another designated field of interest or specialty that you can choose; however, you will not be awarded an additional degree for this course work.

**Off campus housing:** This term refers to any housing that is not provided by the university.

**Pledging:** Pledging is the initial period of joining a Greek organization (fraternity or sorority). Pledging often involves learning facts and the history of one's chosen Greek organization and a variety of activities designed to introduce one to the current members of one's Greek organization.

**RA:** Resident Advisor — is the upperclassman (typically a junior or senior) who is living on your floor in your dorm. RAs often plan various hall or floor activities to help introduce students to each other and also as breaks during the academic year.

**Room Draw/Housing Lottery:** The housing lottery is the process by which dorm rooms are selected for the next academic year. If you choose to live in university-sponsored housing, you will be randomly assigned a number that designates when you can choose housing. When your number comes up in selection, you can then choose from the available housing. Ways to get around the housing lottery may be requesting block housing (a large portion of rooms in the same location of a dorm) or being "pulled in" to another room. When you are "pulled in," someone who chooses housing before you can also request that you are placed into that dorm option.

**Rush:** Rush is the period during which Greek organizations select members. During the first round of rush, students visit with several sororities or fraternities of their choice. However, for the subsequent rounds, the Greek organizations select who is invited back to get to know their organizations. At the end of rush, Greek organizations will extend "bids" to students that they feel would be good matches for their organization. During "bid day" (typically a sorority event) students decide which organization they will join and are welcomed to that organization by its members.

**Semester System:** The semester system divides the academic year into two portions (semesters), typically September to December and then January to May. Courses last for one semester and one's GPA is determined by end of semester grades.

**Student ID:** Your student ID is a plastic card, similar to a credit card with your photo and student ID number on the front, and a metallic swipe strip on the back. The swipe strip can function to let you into a variety of university buildings, such as your dorm, the library and cafeterias (based upon your selected meal plan). In addition, students can deposit money onto their student ID card and swipe the card to pay for things on campus, such as coffee, printing and photocopies. Your student ID card is often your ticket into university events and can get you discounts at a variety of places off campus, such as the movie theater.

**TA:** Teaching Assistant — typically an undergraduate student who has taken the course and done well, or a graduate student who is working with the professor and familiar with the course material. TAs may be assigned to your classes; they can help teach class, run review sessions and may help grade coursework. TAs can be important resources when the professor is not available for course help.

**Undergraduate:** Refers to any student in college for a bachelor's degree.

# NOTES

# APPENDIX

**From Chapter 1:**
*Get Organized and Be Prepared...page 3*

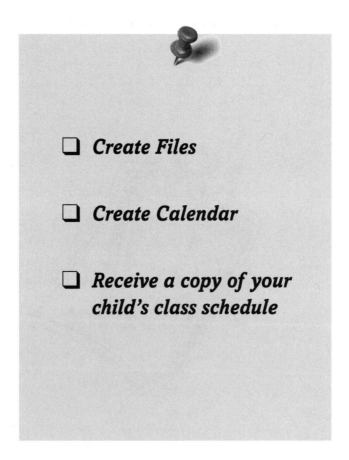

❏ *Create Files*

❏ *Create Calendar*

❏ *Receive a copy of your child's class schedule*

# CREATE A YEARLY CALENDAR
# THAT LISTS...

Move into Dorms/Housing _____

First Day of School _____

Parents Weekend _____

Thanksgiving Vacation _____

First Semester Final Exam Dates_____

Semester Break _____

Second Semester Begins_____

Spring Break _____

Second Semester Final Exam Dates _____

Last Day of School _____

Date Tuition Checks Due — 1st Semester _____

2nd Semester _____

Other Important Dates _____

_____

_____

_____

_____

# STUDENT'S SCHEDULE

| | MONDAY | TUESDAY | WEDNESDAY |
|---|---|---|---|
| 8:00 AM | | | |
| 9:00 | | | |
| 10:00 | | | |
| 11:00 | | | |
| 12:00 PM | | | |
| 1:00 | | | |
| 2:00 | | | |
| 3:00 | | | |
| 4:00 | | | |
| 5:00 | | | |
| 6:00 | | | |
| 7:00 | | | |
| 8:00 | | | |
| 9:00 | | | |
| 10:00 | | | |

FEEL FREE TO COPY THIS PAGE

# STUDENT'S SCHEDULE

| THURSDAY | FRIDAY | SATURDAY | SUNDAY | |
|---|---|---|---|---|
| | | | | 8:00 AM |
| | | | | 9:00 |
| | | | | 10:00 |
| | | | | 11:00 |
| | | | | 12:00 PM |
| | | | | 1:00 |
| | | | | 2:00 |
| | | | | 3:00 |
| | | | | 4:00 |
| | | | | 5:00 |
| | | | | 6:00 |
| | | | | 7:00 |
| | | | | 8:00 |
| | | | | 9:00 |
| | | | | 10:00 |

FEEL FREE TO COPY THIS PAGE

**From Chapter 2:**
*College Paperwork and Forms...page 13*

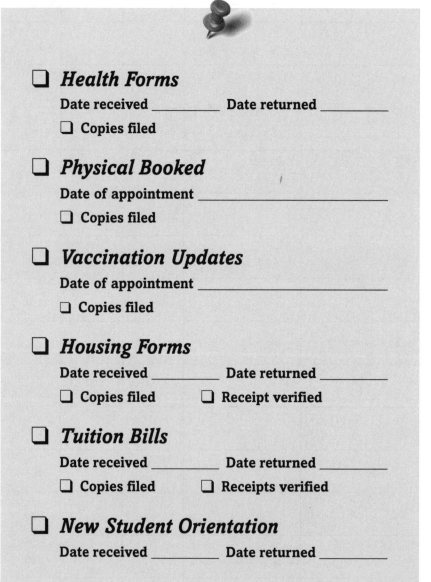

❏ *Health Forms*

Date received _____ Date returned _____

❏ Copies filed

❏ *Physical Booked*

Date of appointment _____

❏ Copies filed

❏ *Vaccination Updates*

Date of appointment _____

❏ Copies filed

❏ *Housing Forms*

Date received _____ Date returned _____

❏ Copies filed       ❏ Receipt verified

❏ *Tuition Bills*

Date received _____ Date returned _____

❏ Copies filed       ❏ Receipts verified

❏ *New Student Orientation*

Date received _____ Date returned _____

**From Chapter 3: *Health...page 23***

❑ *Student ID #* _____

❑ *Student Health Center at College*

    **Phone Number** _____

❑ *Nearest Hospital to College*

    **Name** _____

    **Address** _____

    _____

    _____

    **Phone Number** _____

❑ *Child's Family Doctor*

    **Phone Number** _____

    **Address** _____

    _____

    _____

❑ *Child's Blood Type*

    _____

## ❑ *Nearest Pharmacy*

**Phone Number** _____

**Fax Number** _____

**Address** _____

**Name of any prescription(s) being taken and refills available:**

_____

_____

_____

_____

_____

## ❑ *Child's Eyeglass Prescription*

_____

_____

_____

✳ Plan on transferring any prescriptions before they either expire or run out.

✳ Any special allergies or medical conditions should be discussed.

# ROUTINE VACCINATION RECORD

## *Required for all students:*

| VACCINATION | DOSE | DATE |
| --- | --- | --- |
| Diptheria, Pertussis and Tetanus Tdap or Td booster given within the last **10** years | | |
| Hepatitis B *(3 doses required)* | Dose 1 | |
| | Dose 2 *(given 30 days after the first dose)* | |
| | Dose 3 *(given 4-6 months after the first dose)* | |
| Measles, Mumps, and Rubella *(2 doses required)* | Dose 1 | |
| | Dose 2 | |
| Varicella *(2 doses required)* | Dose 1 | |
| | Dose 2 *(given 4-8 weeks after the first dose)* | |
| **OR** Varicella serological immunity/titer | | |

# ROUTINE VACCINATION RECORD
## *continued*

| VACCINATION | DOSE | DATE |
|---|---|---|
| Haemophilus Influenza *(type B)* | | |
| Polio Vaccination | | |
| Vaccine Prophylactic | | |
| Meningitis | | |
| Gardasil | Dose1 | |
| | Dose 2 | |
| | Dose3 | |

*The yellow International Certificate of Vaccination form is a convenient way to keep track of this information.*

**From Chapter 4: Insurance...*page 35***

## ❏ *Car Insurance*

**New Documentation**_____

_____

**Verified Policy** _____

**Received** _____

## ❏ *Health Insurance*

**New Documentation**_____

_____

**Verified Policy** _____

**Received** _____

## ❏ *Homeowner's Insurance*

**New Documentation**_____

_____

**Verified Policy** _____

**Received** _____

**From Chapter 5:** *Financing and Student Budgeting...page 39*

❏ *Discuss Finances*

❏ *Make a Budget*

❏ *Open a Credit Card/Debit Card*

❏ *Open a Checking Account*

    ❏ Student knows how to write a check

    ❏ Student knows how to make a deposit

    ❏ Student knows how to keep a register

    ❏ Student knows how to reconcile statements

    ❏ Discuss with your child the risks of having credit and identity theft.

FEEL FREE TO COPY THIS PAGE

# FINANCES/STUDENTS BUDGETING THEIR FINANCES

## BUDGET

### INCOME

*List all income available to you from all sources.*

ONE-TIME INCOME:

Scholarships/Awards ..................................................... $_____

Grants ........................................................................... $_____

Monetary gifts .............................................................. $_____

Personal savings ........................................................... $_____

Federal Loans ............................................................... $_____

Private Loans ................................................................ $_____

Other ............................................................................ $_____

SUBTOTAL ONE-TIME INCOME $_____

MONTHLY INCOME:

Salary/Work Wages ....................................................... $_____

Allotment/Allowance .................................................... $_____

Stipend ......................................................................... $_____

Other ............................................................................ $_____

SUBTOTAL MONTHLY INCOME $_____

### TOTAL INCOME $_____

## BUDGET

# EXPENDITURES

## ONE-TIME EXPENSES PER SEMESTER

*School related:*

Tuition .......................................................... $_____

Room .......................................................... $_____

Board (Meal Plan) ....................................... $_____

Athletic Pass ............................................... $_____

Books and Supplies ..................................... $_____

Fees ........................................................... $_____

Fraternity/Sorority Expenses ..................... $_____

Lab Fees ..................................................... $_____

Parking Permit ........................................... $_____

Transportation (Passes) ............................. $_____

Other .......................................................... $_____

*Other one-time expenses:*

Cable/Internet Deposit ............................... $_____

Car Insurance ............................................. $_____

Computers .................................................. $_____

Dorm Supplies/Linens ................................ $_____

Furniture .................................................... $_____

Health Insurance ........................................ $_____

Renter's Insurance ...................................... $_____

Telephone Deposit ....................................... $_____

SUBTOTAL ONE-TIME EXPENSES $_____

FEEL FREE TO COPY THIS PAGE

## BUDGET

# EXPENDITURES

MONTHLY EXPENSES:

*Housing:*

Rent ................................................................... $_____

Cable/Internet .................................................... $_____

Newspaper/Magazines ......................................... $_____

Telephone .......................................................... $_____

Utilities .............................................................. $_____

Other ................................................................. $_____

*Household:*

Food................................................................... $_____

Dry Cleaning ...................................................... $_____

Laundry .............................................................. $_____

Medications ........................................................ $_____

Toiletries ............................................................ $_____

Other ................................................................. $_____

*Transportation:*

Bus/Subway Fare ................................................ $_____

Car Loan ............................................................. $_____

Car Maintenance ................................................ $_____

Gasoline .............................................................. $_____

Parking ............................................................... $_____

SUBTOTAL MONTHLY EXPENSES $_____

## BUDGET

## EXPENDITURES

MONTHLY EXPENSES:

*Recreation:*

Eating Out ................................................. $_____

Entertainment .......................................... $_____

Trips ........................................................ $_____

Other ....................................................... $_____

*Clothing:* ........................................................ $_____

*Gifts:* ............................................................. $_____

*Monthly Payments:*

Credit Cards ............................................ $_____

Membership Dues .................................... $_____

SUBTOTAL MONTHLY EXPENSES  $_____

SUBTOTAL MONTHLY EXPENSES *(from page 176)* $_____

## TOTAL MONTHLY EXPENSES $_____

SUBTOTAL ONE-TIME EXPENSES *(from page 177)* $_____

## TOTAL EXPENSES $_____

## TOTAL INCOME *(from page 175)* $_____

**From Chapter 6: Dorm Rooms...*page 63***

❑ *Check homeowner's policy for coverage*

❑ *Secure additional insurance riders if needed*

❑ *Fill in personal property inventory list*

❑ *Fill in inventory list*

❑ *Check for store sales, shop and start packing*

➡ Label boxes as you pack them, it'll make it easier when you load your car and then have to unpack.

➡ Pack the fragile items in between linens. Kate used pillows to wrap around TV and computer screens

➡ Office supply stores usually have school supplies on sale in July.

FEEL FREE TO COPY THIS PAGE

# PERSONAL PROPERTY INVENTORY LIST

| Item | Description | Model # |
|------|-------------|---------|
| Bicycle | | |
| Camera | | |
| Cell Phone | | |
| Computer & Peripheral Equipment | | |
| iPod | | |
| Musical instrument | | |
| Stereo/ DVD | | |
| TV | | |
| Other | | |
| | | |
| | | |
| | | |
| | | |

| Purchase Serial # | Warranty Date | Expires | $ Value |
|---|---|---|---|
| | | | |
| | | | |
| | | | |
| | | | |
| | | | |
| | | | |
| | | | |
| | | | |
| | | | |
| | | | |
| | | | |
| | | | |
| | SUBTOTAL | | |

*Use this inventory checklist to record additional personal property.*

# INVENTORY CHECKLIST

| Items | $ Value |
|---|---|
| CDs & DVDs | |
| Clothes/Shoes | |
| Electrical items *(printers, radio, hairdryer, etc.)* | |
| | |
| | |
| | |
| | |
| | |
| Furniture | |
| Jewelry | |
| | |
| | |
| **SUBTOTAL** | |

# INVENTORY CHECKLIST

| Items | $ Value |
|---|---|
| Linens | |
| Photo/Film Gear | |
| Sports Equipment | |
| | |
| | |
| Text Books | |
| Other | |
| | |
| Add $1,000 for unlisted items | $1,000 |
| **SUBTOTAL** *(page 180)* | |
| **SUBTOTAL** *(page 181)* | |
| **SUBTOTAL** *(page 182)* | |
| **TOTAL** *(pages 180-183)* | |

# WHAT SHOULD YOUR CHILD TAKE

The following is a list containing almost everything that you could think of to bring. Use it as a guide and once again **plan on taking only what you need**. *REMEMBER whatever you take will have to either be stored or come back home with you at the end of the semester.*

## Linens

❑ 2 extra-long sheet sets *(flat sheet, fitted sheet and 2 pillow cases)*

❑ 1 extra-long mattress pad (mattress dimension is — *36" x 6" x 80"*)

❑ 1 extra-long egg crate pad or fiberbed/featherbed to soften an uncomfortable mattress

❑ 1 comforter *(washable since you'll spend most of your time on it)*

❑ 2 pillows

❑ 1 fleece blanket *(can purchase at school)*

❑ 2 bath sheets *(extra large towels)*

❑ 1 hand towel

❑ 1 wash cloth

## Room, Closet and Storage

❑ Bed lifts or rack risers ✳
❑ Bookcase/shelving unit
❑ Clear plastic boxes
❑ Collapsible folding crate
❑ Door mirror
❑ Drawer liners/shelf paper
❑ Drawer organizers
❑ Extension cords
❑ Floor lamps
❑ Hangers and add-on multiple hangers
❑ Jewelry organizer
❑ Night light
❑ Over-door hooks
❑ "S" hooks
❑ Table lamps
❑ Under-bed drawers ✳

✳ *Usually you have 3-4 dresser drawers and a reasonable size closet. You may want to raise the bed and utilize the space underneath for additional storage.*

## Cleaning/Laundry

- ❑ Broom & dust pan
- ❑ Cleaning supplies
- ❑ Clothes hamper
- ❑ Drying rack
- ❑ Goo Gone
- ❑ Iron and portable ironing board *(optional — most students will never use)*

- ❑ Laundry basket with name on it
- ❑ Lint brush
- ❑ Paper towels, tissues, etc.
- ❑ Portable vacuum cleaner
- ❑ Stain remover
- ❑ Wrinkle-free spray

## Eating/Cooking*

- ❑ Airtight food storage containers
- ❑ Bowls
- ❑ Can/bottle opener
- ❑ Chip clips
- ❑ Coffee/travel mugs
- ❑ Cups
- ❑ Ice cube trays
- ❑ Magnetic paper towel holder and paper towels
- ❑ Microfridge *(microwave/refrigerator combo)*

- ❑ Microwave-safe food containers
- ❑ Plates
- ❑ Quart size plastic bags
- ❑ Salt and pepper shakers
- ❑ Silverware
- ❑ Water filtering pitcher and replacement filters

✳ *For your late night snacks you'll want to have on hand a supply of packages of sugar, sweeteners, ketchup, mayonnaise and mustard.*

## Electronics

- All in one printer/scanner/copier
- Backup software
- Batteries
- Cable cord
- CD-Rs
- Computer *(college may offer discounts)*
- Computer screen *(unless you have a laptop)*
- Digital camera
- DVD player
- Ethernet cord
- Extension cord
- Inkjet cartridges
- Jump drive
- Mouse pad
- MP3 player
- Power strip/surge protector
- Television
- Wireless card

## Must Haves

- Alarm clock/clock radio
- Cell phone
- Compact umbrella
- Duffle/overnight bag
- Fan
- First aid kit *(see page 33)*

## Sewing Kit*

- Pins
- Buttons
- Thread
- Sewing needles

\* *There are some wonderful hotel sewing kits that contain almost everything that your child will need and already have the needles threaded with various colored threads.*

\* *Chances are that your child will not be mending anything — but every now and then a button falls off that will need to be replaced.*

*Remember that dry cleaners often can mend and hem for a nominal charge.*

## Showering

- ❑ Bath robe
- ❑ Cosmetics & toiletries
- ❑ Flip flops
- ❑ Hair dryer
- ❑ Mirror
- ❑ Over-door towel rack
- ❑ Plastic cup
- ❑ Soap container
- ❑ Toiletries
- ❑ Toothbrush holder
- ❑ Waterproof shower caddy

## Studying and Office Supplies

- ❑ Backpack or book bag
- ❑ Binders
- ❑ Book ends
- ❑ Bulletin boards for desk and pushpins
- ❑ Calculator
- ❑ CD/DVD organizers
- ❑ Copy paper
- ❑ Cord/cable organizers
- ❑ Desk lamp and light bulbs
- ❑ Desk organizers
- ❑ Drawer organizers
- ❑ Duct tape
- ❑ Glue stick
- ❑ Hole punch
- ❑ Index cards
- ❑ Invisible hanging wire
- ❑ Laptop carrying case
- ❑ Message board for dorm room door
- ❑ Notebooks
- ❑ Paper clips
- ❑ Pen & pencil holder
- ❑ Pencil sharpener
- ❑ Pencils, pens
- ❑ Picture frames
- ❑ Post-it® notes
- ❑ Removable mounting tape
- ❑ Ruler
- ❑ Scissors
- ❑ Stackable desk trays
- ❑ Stapler
- ❑ Storage units
- ❑ Tape
- ❑ Trash can
- ❑ Velcro

## Tool Kit

- ❑ Duct tape
- ❑ Flashlight
- ❑ Flat head screwdriver
- ❑ Hammer with a claw
- ❑ Nails
- ❑ Phillip's head screwdriver
- ❑ Pliers with wire cutters
- ❑ Putty knife
- ❑ Screws
- ❑ Steel Wool
- ❑ Tape measure
- ❑ Utility knife with retractable blade

**From Chapter 7:**
*New Student Orientations...page 75*

❏ *Received new student orientation information*

❏ *Registered for:*_____

❏ *Responded on:* _____

❏ *Payment:* _____

❏ *Booked / reserved hotel or dorm rooms*

❏ *Arranged for transportion to college*

**From Chapter 9: Settling In...***page 93*

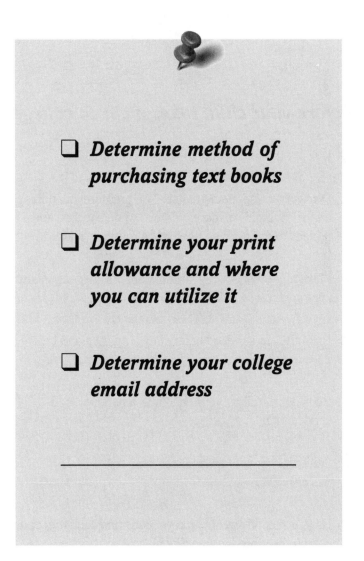

❏ *Determine method of purchasing text books*

❏ *Determine your print allowance and where you can utilize it*

❏ *Determine your college email address*

**From Chapter 10:**
*Cars on Campus...page 99*

# *Before your child takes a car to college*

❑ Discuss the practicality of this.

❑ Discuss routine maintenance. Tire pressure, oil, fluids and windshield washer fluid need to be checked and replenished. Cars also need to be routinely started.

❑ Make a copy of the registration, date of inspection and insurance cards to keep at home.

❑ Have the car serviced before any long trips and before it goes to school.

❑ Consider enrolling your child into a national road service plan.

❑ Stock the car with a Car Emergency Kit *(see page 192)*.

❑ Have a second set of car keys made and sent with your child to be stored in a secure place.

FEEL FREE TO COPY THIS PAGE

❏ Check with your auto insurance policy. Since the car will be in a new location for at least eight months, this might make a difference in your premiums. It is important that the company be notified that the car will be kept at another location, should anything happen.

❏ Locate a mechanic or service station before you need them. If possible, find a National Institute for Automotive Service Excellence mechanic.

FEEL FREE TO COPY THIS PAGE

# CAR EMERGENCY KIT

## BASIC TOOL KIT
*(adjustable wrench, pliers, screwdrivers and wrenches)*

Car jack

Cellular phone charger

Disposable camera
*(to take photos when involved in a fender-bender)*

Emergency flares, warning triangle, or cones

Fire extinguisher

First aid kit

Flashlight

Insurance and emergency phone numbers

Jumper cables

Paper towels

Pressurized can of tire inflator and sealer
for emergency filling of a flat tire

Windshield washer fluid

## FOR WINTER MONTHS
Ice scraper and snowbrush

Kitty litter great for traction when stuck
in snow/mud

Mini shovel

## From Chapter 11: Travel and Transportation...*page 107*

✱ *Sign your child up now for frequent flyer programs.*

# AIRLINES

| AIRLINES | | Frequent Flyer # | Pin # |
|---|---|---|---|
| Air Canada | www.aircanada.com<br>1-888-247-2262 | | |
| AirTran | www.airtran.com<br>1-800-247-8726 | | |
| American Airlines | www.aa.com<br>1-800-433-7300 | | |
| American Trans Air | www.ata.com<br>1-800-225-2995 | | |
| British Airways | www.britishairways.com<br>1-800-247-9297 | | |
| Continental Airlines | www.continental.com<br>1-800-525-0280 | | |
| Delta Air Lines | www.delta.com<br>1-800-221-1212 | | |
| JetBlue Airways | www.jetblue.com<br>1-800-538-2583 | | |
| Northwest Airlines | www.nwa.com<br>1-800-225-2525 | | |
| Southwest Airlines | www.southwest.com<br>1-800-435-9792 | | |
| Ted Airlines | www.flyted.com<br>1-800-225-5833 | | |
| United Airlines | www.united.com<br>1-800-241-6522 | | |
| USAir | www.usairways.com<br>1-800-428-4322 | | |
| | | | |

## Packing a Suitcase

### Essentials that will fit into one 22" suitcase
2 pairs of pants and 2 pairs of shorts

4 shirts and blouses or 4 t-shirts/tank tops

One nice jacket/tie or dress/nice pants and top

Pajamas/nightgown/nightshirt

One turtleneck

Long sleeved shirt

Sweater or fleece

Underwear & socks *(no more than a total of 7)*

Waterproof jacket, raincoat or foldable umbrella

Bathing suit

Flip-flops

Dress shoes

Cap/visor

Hairbrush, comb and toothbrush

Toothpaste, Deodorant, Shampoo, Conditioner
*(sometimes provided if staying in hotels,
otherwise purchase mini versions)*

Contact lens solution, Cosmetics

Shaving cream and razor

Insect repellant/Sunscreen
*(pack everything in leak-proof plastic bags to contain any spillage)*

***REMEMBER, IF YOU TAKE THESE ON BOARD A PLANE, EACH
MUST BE 2 OUNCES OR LESS
AND FIT INTO A QUART-SIZE BAG.***

### *Wear onboard*
Hooded sweatshirt or sweater

Sneakers/heavy shoes

FEEL FREE TO COPY THIS PAGE

**From Chapter 12:**
**Odds and Ends...***page 115*

❏ *Discuss alcohol and*
*drug use*

❏ *Discuss how to do*
*laundry*

❏ *Demonstrate some*
*basic sewing skills*
*if necessary*

❏ *Discuss the practice of*
*tipping for services*
*rendered*

## From Chapter 13:
### *Book Your Hotel Rooms Now...page 123*

## *Date*

_____ **Parents Weekend**
- ❏ Hotel reservations made
  Confirmation #: _____
- ❏ Travel plans made


_____ **Last Day of Classes/Move Out Day**
- ❏ Hotel reservations made
  Confirmation #: _____
- ❏ Travel plans made

_____ **First Day of Next Year/Move In Day**
- ❏ Hotel reservations made
  Confirmation #: _____
- ❏ Travel plans made

_____ **Graduation**
- ❏ Hotel reservations made
  Confirmation #: _____
- ❏ Travel plans made

# *OTHER SPECIAL DAYS*

## *Date*

_____ **Athletic Event** _____
- ❑ Hotel reservations made
  Confirmation #: _____
- ❑ Travel plans made

_____ **Athletic Event** _____
- ❑ Hotel reservations made
  Confirmation #: _____
- ❑ Travel plans made

_____ **Athletic Event** _____
- ❑ Hotel reservations made
  Confirmation #: _____
- ❑ Travel plans made

_____ **Athletic Event** _____
- ❑ Hotel reservations made
  Confirmation #: _____
- ❑ Travel plans made

**From Chapter 14:**
*Sending Items to Your Child...page 133*

## *Address and Phone Number*

**Where packages can be sent:**

_____

_____

Phone _____

**Where Saturday or Sunday next day mail can be sent and RECEIVED**

_____

_____

Phone _____

**Nearest FedEx/Kinko's:**

_____

_____

Phone _____

## *List of Special Occasions*

_____

_____

_____

_____

_____

_____

## *Supplies*

❑ *Address labels*

❑ *Boxes*

❑ *Commercial grade tape*

❑ *Contents (food, etc.)*

# NOTES

# INDEX

# INDEX

# NOTES

# NOTES

# NOTES

# NOTES

# NOTES